THE
MYSTERY
METHOD

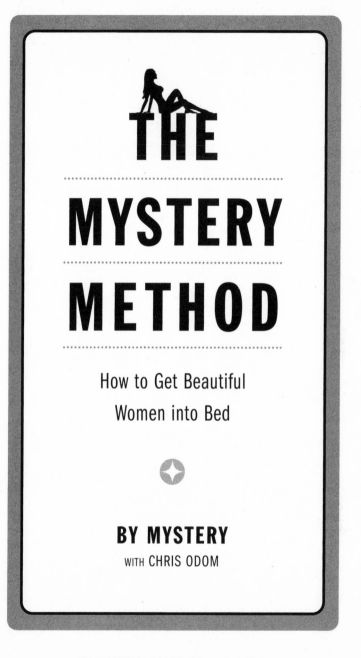

THE
MYSTERY
METHOD

How to Get Beautiful
Women into Bed

BY MYSTERY
WITH CHRIS ODOM

ST. MARTIN'S PRESS 🏵 NEW YORK

www.stmartins.com

BOOK DESIGN BY AMANDA DEWEY

Library of Congress Cataloging-in-Publication Data
Mystery.
    The Mystery method : how to get beautiful women into bed / Mystery; foreword by Neil Strauss.
        p.   cm.
    ISBN-13: 978-0-312-36011-5
    ISBN-10: 0-312-36011-8
    1. Dating (social customs).   2. Mate selections.   3. Single women—Psychology.   4. Single men—Psychology.   I. Title.

HQ801.M97   2006
646.7'7—dc22   2006050645

10   9

*I have dedicated my life to exploring
and understanding humanity.*

*The Mystery Method is my humble yet ambitious attempt
to solve the greatest mystery in the universe:*

women.

This work is compassionately dedicated to them.

CONTENTS

FOREWORD

Hey, man."

    That's how it always begins. And then he will say, in return, "Hey, man."

And then one of us will say, "I'm tired."

And the other will say, "I don't feel like going out today."

"Neither do I."

That's how it always begins—with feet, minds, hearts dragging. That's never how it ends.

"We'll just go get some food."

"Okay, just something quick. I'm really tired."

"We've covered that already."

"And I look like shit."

"I noticed."

"Shut up." Playful punch to the arm.

Pull in to the parking lot. It is sushi night. Every night is sushi night.

Two women walk past, probably college students. We try not to notice, but the smell of peach-scented moisturizer lingers in the air after them. It is too much for us. It sends us over the edge.

A smile creeps over his lips, color rises to his cheeks, his eyes begin to glitter mischievously.

"Is that your set or mine?" he asks.

"I thought we weren't going to sarge tonight."

"I know. But look at them. You're Style. Fucking Style, man! What would the boys say if you just let them go like that?"

"Yeah, but you're Mystery. You invented this shit. Let's see your stuff. Let's see if you still have it."

They disappear into a Chinese restaurant.

"Oh well, they're gone. Let's go get some sushi."

"This is even better. Now they're not moving targets."

"Okay, fine. I'll do this quickly—for you, fucker."

"I'll be there in a few, to wing you."

One of us begins the slow, reluctant, weary trudge into the Chinese restaurant. He pretends as if he's walking to the bathroom, then suddenly pivots as he starts to pass the table with the girls. Deep breath. Smile. Head turns back over shoulder. Now it is time—time to toss a casual, offhand question their way, any of a number you can read about in this book.

The women respond with middling interest. This is to be expected. It is part of the game.

The next part is to pretend to leave but then, as an afterthought, make a small observation or comment or question. They take the bait. They always do. Now it is time to hook them—with the personality we've carefully cultivated, with the illusions we've spent months refining, with any of a number of other techniques that also lie in these pages—our master plan, now your master plan.

Hooked. They are hooked. Not like fish, but like new friends. This is the moment; this is what the game is all about. This is the high you get when these two complete strangers who you've approached don't want you to leave.

That's when the other will come in from outside, feigning innocence. Accomplishment intro him before he reaches the table. They approve. He introduces himself, displaying that winning personality cobbled from thousands of approaches. We sit down with them at the table, but only for a moment, we explain. The time constraint is key. We use it liberally.

It seems we are having Chinese tonight. Our meals are not ours to determine. We must go with the flow, the flow of peach moisturizer or fall-leaves perfume or vanilla talcum powder or rose-petal conditioner. This is what we do. This is what we must do. We are not just men, we are Venusian artists. It is our calling. These sweet-smelling beings are bored. They need adventure. They need our sparkling personalities and pre-scripted value demonstrations and comfort-building routines and last-minute-resistance stories and dual-induction massages and secret-spot orgasm techniques. We need their feminine energy. It's our gasoline.

No, we are not tired anymore. We are fully awake. Wide awake and in the game. This is life. This is living. This is what we were put on this earth for, making these two girls laugh. It is music from heaven. And learning to make that music is what this book is about.

We leave with phone numbers pressed into our palms.

At least that's what happened this time, because it's a true story. The most recent one. In the old days, we would have invited them out that night with us or at least followed up and called them. But now we are too busy. Our lives are already full of intrigues. We make them complicated on purpose. We see how ridiculous we can get—how far we can push the line of what is socially acceptable, sexually possible, romantically inconceivable. We enjoy the drama. We don't always enjoy the consequences. But we survive them to live and love another day.

Our lives weren't always like this. They were once free of consequences, free of drama, free of love, and free of women. But we weren't free. We were a slave to our desire, to the knowledge that there were guys out there who had dates and girlfriends and fun. We didn't. We watched them. We tried to figure out what they had and we didn't.

People yearn to be creative. They think that this means they must go into acting, writing, visual art, or music. But there are other arts. Cooking can be an art. So can boxing. Mystery's is social dynamics. He can play a room like Eric Clapton can play a guitar. Not like Jimi Hendrix, but like Eric Clapton.

When I learned this art, I studied at the feet of the masters. When Mystery learned it, he didn't know about masters. He didn't know there was an art. It was pure. He studied human behavior. For years. Until slowly he put it together. The charts. The diagrams. The algorithms. The technical terms. Every day, he wrapped his head around the puzzle of social interaction. Until he put together every piece. Elegantly. Neatly. Like Eric Clapton. And I don't even listen to Eric Clapton anymore. I think he's sometimes overrated. Mystery's not. Not yet. He will be one day, when pickup becomes the new workout and pumping emotions the new pumping iron.

Watching him work was the day my life changed, the day that I realized that the disease of loneliness had a cure.

That cure is the Mystery Method.

Welcome to your new lifestyle. Are you tired yet?

—Neil Strauss

PREFACE

Nature will unapologetically weed your genes out of existence if you don't take action and learn how to attract women now.

Do I have your attention?

Good, because attracting women is a serious matter. You agree with this statement, or you wouldn't have picked up this book in the first place. But just because it's a matter of life and death doesn't mean the process of attracting women can't be superfun!

If you want to be a multimillionaire, you need a proven game plan for accumulating wealth, right? If you want to look like an Adonis, you need a proven game plan for sculpting your physique, too. Well, what if you want to have beautiful women, the kind you see in magazine spreads and music videos, on your arm and in your bed? In that case, the Mystery Method (MM) is your proven game plan for creating a lifestyle filled with unlimited choices. I created it, and if you'll allow me the privilege, I'll be your personal mentor to see that you learn it thoroughly.

It's no secret I've dated some of the most beautiful women in the world, and for that I make no apologies (although physical beauty is but one of many qualities I look for in a female companion). Now, I've never thought of myself as a pickup artist, nor should you, but it was always flattering to have friends ask me how I acquired such stunning girlfriends. So, informally, I began to teach them my secret of attraction. Armed with this knowledge, soon they, too, had beautiful girl-friends.

May the Venusian arts enrich your life,
not define it.

MYSTERY

Over the years, these informal discussions with friends evolved into dynamic seminars and action-packed workshops conducted "in the field." I literally brought men into nightclubs and other social settings and trained them on the spot in how to systematically approach and attract women. I personally have helped thousands of men all over the world learn what their dads never taught them.

That is why I am privileged to share with you more than ten years of experience in the science of social dynamics and the art of the cold-approach pickup. My goal with the Mystery Method is to accelerate your learning curve dramatically, saving you years of painful frustration and loneliness in the process.

Seek the path to Venusian arts mastery.

Love,

Mystery

mystery@themysterymethod.com

P.S. Make sure to check out my concluding letter on page 209 for details on how to best use this book to achieve the lifestyle with beautiful women that you want. Also, be sure to check out our companion Web site at www.getattraction.com.

If you can't attract a woman, you are,
by dictionary definition, sterile.

MYSTERY

THE
MYSTERY
METHOD

···

THE MYSTERY BEHIND CASANOVA

If teachers and parents taught subjects in their order of importance to the males receiving their "wisdom," history lessons wouldn't invoke Greek philosophers and ancient mystics, presidents and kings, warriors and generals. They would focus instead on Casanova, history's most accomplished and successful lover. He was born in Venice, Italy, in 1725, and he died in 1798, numbers that are less important than these: By his own account, over those seventy-three years, Casanova enjoyed erotic liaisons with 122 women during his travels across Europe as a clergyman, soldier, violinist, and magician. In eighteenth-century France, nobody had more game.

But Casanova didn't seduce indiscriminately. He set his sights high and took to bed only those women whose value made them worthy of pickup. These were the perfect 10s and near 10s of their day: what a *Sports Illustrated* swimsuit model might have looked like at one of Mozart's recitals, floating from one social set to the next, glancing discreetly over a ruffled fan that obscured a plunging bustline, her hairdo intricately sculpted three feet high. They were women of extreme beauty with the highest social ranking, seemingly off-limits to anyone but royalty.

Forget Shakespeare's sonnets, the Gettysburg Address, and *War and Peace*—if Casanova had left behind not just an autobiography (itself wildly popular to this day) but a step-by-step, detailed how-to guide to his sexual conquests, it would rank as the most sought-after text in history, next to Holy Scriptures.

What wouldn't you or any man give to learn the secret of seducing beautiful women? Just look at the timeless appeal of the Kama Sutra—and then imagine a guide not to exotic sexual positions but to getting beautiful women attracted to you in the first place.

My name is Mystery, and I have written just such a guide, now in your hands. As the world's premier pickup artist, I am the closest thing there is to a modern-day Casanova (although I have already "outnumbered" him). Like my predecessor, I absolutely adore women. In fact, I fall in love with all of them. But that doesn't make me unique. What makes me unique is that because of the pickup techniques I have mastered, my love doesn't go unrequited. And I'm here to show you how to achieve the same success.

THE ALGORITHM FOR GETTING WOMEN

Not only were the Venusian arts (the arts of love) excluded from your curriculum—but they're probably the only discipline teachers didn't try to cram into your brain as you passed from childhood through adolescence and then into adulthood. Let's face it, when you studied algebra at school, the only numbers you really cared about were the measurements of the girl in the tight sweater and the digits you needed to get her on the phone. Those numbers added up to something worth getting your hands on.

Enter the Mystery Method. If someone doesn't have health and wants to get it, he or she will need to adopt an algorithm on how to do that—perhaps a new diet and workout regimen. If someone doesn't have wealth and wants to get it, he or she will need to adopt an algorithm for wealth building—perhaps a new investment portfolio. Similarly, in relationships, if someone doesn't have success and wants to get it, he or she will need to adopt the algorithm for success there. I invented that algorithm.

I am your teacher and this is your guidebook to discerning the patterns in dynamic social interactions and then using them to your advantage. This body of knowledge, called the science of social dynamics, has become my life's work, particularly as it applies to the world of pickup. It is about more than seduction and sexual conquest; it also encompasses making friends with men and women alike. But, make no mistake, it is first and foremost about getting laid more than you could ever have dreamed possible, assuming that's what you want. And not just laid but, like Casanova, laid by those gorgeous women who have always seemed beyond reach. For him, it was members of the aristocracy; for you, I'm talking about the women you see walking runways in stiletto heels, on the arms of pro athletes and celebrities, and in the pages of *Playboy* and *Maxim*. You can have them. The Mystery Method can give them to you.

MASTERING THE SCIENCE OF COURTSHIP

The Mystery Method provides a step-by-step game plan that structures "courtship"—which is the quaint, old-fashioned term for the sequence of events that results in guys getting laid—for success. Before me, no one had ever defined courtship as a predetermined structure having several phases. Through years of study and experimentation, I identified a process that begins when you meet a woman who interests you. From there, using a finely calibrated ability to influence (not manipulate; there's a huge difference), which this book will help you develop, you build attraction with her. This concept is hugely important: Attraction comes before seduction. But attraction, while necessary, isn't an end in itself. Next, you need to build comfort with this woman you've targeted. (As you'll find out, both are equally necessary for reaching the end-game: sex.) As I teach "courtship," the process of building attraction and comfort will probably transpire over several venues—say, a bar and a restaurant—en route to the final venue, which will likely be your bed, or a hotel room's. That won't happen, however, until you create arousal at the end of the comfort-building stage and then begin a sexual relationship by seducing her.

That's what the Mystery Method does. What it is, is an advanced algorithm thirteen years in the making. I created it through years of trial and error, because I had to. When I was starting out there was no guidebook like the one you have now. I didn't have the luxury of buying a book like this, or attending a seminar, or Googling "pickup artist" online. Armed with nothing but ignorance and desire, I went out into "the field," because that's where the girls were. Step-by-step, I learned first how to "open." Once I learned how to open, I also discovered empirically that in public settings girls of beauty are seldom, if ever, alone. So then I had to get good at opening an entire group, and so on, until my system for seducing women became comprehensive, battle-tested, and turnkey.

Honestly, had I read a guidebook like this when I was starting out, I would have saved myself about seven years of pain and confusion.

Since its conception, the Mystery Method has been modified by some of my closest friends, most of whom were former students of mine who got caught up to speed on my techniques and became great pickup artists in their own right. Just as my students have learned their craft from me, I have in turn learned much from them, and the insights they gained in the field have improved my own methodology. Like any system of self-improvement and personal transformation, the Mystery Method is constantly being improved. It will always be a work in progress because the people using it are constantly changing as well. To keep it up-to-date with the latest empirical data available, I make systematic improvements every six months, without fail. You can keep up with our refinements and new discoveries at www.mysterymethod.com.

UNLOCK THE SECRET TO ATTRACTING BEAUTIFUL WOMEN

If you follow the Mystery Method, as outlined in this book, you literally should be able to seduce any woman you meet—no matter how attractive she is and no matter how far out of reach she seems—within four to ten hours, with the average seduction occurring within seven, leading to what I call the Seven-Hour Rule. (Bear in mind that those seven hours aren't necessarily continuous, although they can be. As I noted, usually taking courtship to seduction requires venue changes, which have to be accommodated through what are called time bridges. More on those later.)

Seducing any woman in seven hours . . . how is this possible? The reason the Mystery Method works, and works so quickly, is that it defines the natural process of courtship, from meeting to sex, that has applied to every love story you've ever heard about, or read, or experienced. It reflects universal truths and the natural course of events, and I've backward-engineered it from my own successes. I would go in, "build" a girlfriend, and then think, *OK, how did I do that?* That's how I figured out and unraveled the myriad of cognitive models that define courtship.

OK, you're probably thinking, *Of course I'd love to build attraction and comfort with a gorgeous woman, but every time I approach one I get shot down before I've finished my second or third sentence.* Here's the deal— and it's one of the most amazing secrets of the Mystery Method because it is so counterintuitive, running contrary to everything you've believed about attracting beautiful women your entire life. In order for you to be permitted the audience of a beautiful woman to attempt to attract her, you must first disqualify yourself from being considered a potential suitor by her. If you don't do that, she will assume **by your approach alone** that you're after her. And if you're after her, she knows that you perceive her as having high value. And if her value is high, the odds are that it's higher than yours. In other words, you will have low value, and you will be penalized, not only just for approaching her but also for being nice. At that point, you've already telegraphed that you're not worth it.

I will teach you how to avoid this trap using the Mystery Method. Instead of stumbling into a group of women blindly and immediately qualifying yourself as a potential suitor, you will learn how to win them over during those first few minutes, allowing you to demonstrate a higher value to them. The book will of course give you chapter and verse on demonstrating a higher value, from "peacocking" (dressing outlandishly) and preselecting (displaying other women to the "tar-

get," which often builds a jealousy plotline into your seduction), to social proof (showing that others in her set value you highly), to "negging"
(making subtle-yet-negative statements that put your target off-guard
and make her question her own value, increasing yours on a relative
basis). There is even a special section on demonstrating higher value
to, and then picking up, "hired guns," a term describing anyone who is
hired for her beauty, including exotic dancers, bartenders, go-go
dancers, hostesses, and models.

In fact, throughout the entire book I fill in the meeting-to-sex structure of courtship with Venusian arts gambits, so that you can complete
the objectives of each phase. But I go further still by adding a third
layer to the book. I show you how to personalize your game, helping
you create and then convey an identity whose stereotype works for
you to presume higher value. The last thing I want to do is turn you
into a generic cookie-cutter pickup artist. Using the Mystery Method,
I picked up a supermodel as she sat with seven coworkers at a popular
Hollywood sushi bar. While they paid the bill, I had only two or three
minutes to interact. I immediately initiated a chat with her, disquali-
fied myself from being considered a potential suitor, and systematically demonstrated my value to her, while not telegraphing interest.
When my target's group left, she decided to hang by the bar with two
friends. To develop social proof, I opened an adjacent four-set—two
girls, two guys—and disarmed the guys, who soon departed. With
two women on my arms, I re-engaged my target, now in a three-set.
Introducing my wing into the set to befriend and occupy my target's
friends for a moment, I moved her into isolation, escalated kino, and
voila! I got my first supermodel.

Once you've mastered the techniques I outline here, you too can
perform equally spectacular seductions!

BUILDING A MYSTERY

I can do it for you because I've done it for myself. Believe it or not,
when I was younger, I was actually an extremely shy person. No won-

der I became fascinated by magic. I loved hiding behind it; it afforded me a social mask, protecting me in my interactions with people. Magic provided me with prescripted routines packing an emotional punch.

The turning point for me came in my late teens, when I traveled to Florida to perform a magic show on a cruise ship. Before I could even get scheduled on the ship, I found myself making more money performing intimate and interactive illusion in restaurants and lounges. In fact, I did so well in the restaurants that I never bothered to make it on board. More important, the experience taught me a series of essential concepts. For example, in that setting, you shouldn't just walk up to a table of strangers and say, "Uh, hi. Would you like to see some magic?" The easiest thing for someone to say in that situation is no. So I had to come up with a series of techniques for being cool—that way, they would actually want me to be there. Then I had to internalize these rules that I developed, so that over repeated days of work I'd get better and better at it. Eventually, I found myself in possession of a really cool social skill set.

Then I came to realize that I could remove the magic from those routines and they would still pack a punch. I got good at developing stories and plotlines with which I could captivate a group, and that became the basis of forming routines and using canned material. I then started teaching these skills to my friends.

They mastered them, and so can you. If you're thinking, *Yeah, that worked for you, but it will never work for me; I'm a geek,* don't worry. I was a geek, too. The truth is, generally speaking, geeks are intelligent individuals who simply haven't yet applied that intelligence to social scenarios; hence, they appear deficient in that area. Making matters worse, the society around us, at first glance, appears very chaotic. But when you look at all other human beings as beautiful, elegant biological machines embedded with sophisticated behavioral systems designed to align with others to maximize their chances for survival and replication, the task of understanding humanity and your place in it becomes surmountable.

Not only was I myself a geek, but I've also taught the Mystery

Method to other geeks! And you know what? They're not geeks any-more, and neither will you be. With me as your friend and guide, you'll start uploading Venusian arts programming into your behavioral sys-tem and then practice and internalize it so you won't have to think about picking up. It will just happen naturally when the moment arises. By reading this book, all you're doing is hanging out with a guy who figured it out. I figured it out. I know how. I know for a fact that I know how because I have a girlfriend.

Along those same lines, this book also will work wonders for you if your relations with women have been hindered by your perception, true or not, that you're physically unattractive. In fact, you have less to worry about than the geek, because the "attraction circuits" of women are calibrated to find a man attractive not measured primarily by handsomeness or physique but rather by social value. It's not as much about looks as it is about conveying that you are the "tribal leader."

Allow me to explain. A woman's job is to survive and replicate. To achieve those ends, she will align herself with anyone who can assist her in that survival and replication. The more S-and-R value the per-son has, the merrier. So the powerful leader of a tribe might be old, fat, and bald, but aligning with him will greatly improve her chances of survival and replication because of his power to protect her. To use a more modern-day analogy, how many times have you seen a gorgeous woman with a brick-house body on the arm of an older, hunched-over man who looks like he would need a forklift to get it up? You and I both know that guy owns a nightclub or some apartment buildings. He sure as hell isn't working at a car wash.

So if you aren't the easiest guy on the eyes, I will show you how to become the "tribal leader" within your own family, community, and circle of friends. Even if it takes you several years to become one . . . that's what you have to be.

If you're not a geek and you're not physically unattractive, but you fail in your efforts to seduce women because you're shy, don't worry. I, too, was shy. One of the great things about the Mystery Method is that, initially at least, you can hide behind stock routines and canned material, using them as tools for social dynamic interaction and the enjoyment of performing lighthearted social experiments. In this way, I will show you how to educate yourself and attain social intelligence.

Being shy just means that you're scared to interact with other people. If you feel lonely, if you feel bad, those emotions exist for a purpose: to motivate you to improve your chances of survival and replication. You do that by aligning with other human beings who have S-and-R value. You're designed for social dynamic interaction; your brain is hardwired for you to be a social robot. Rooted in evolutionary behavioral psychology, the Mystery Method will help you align with your brain's design and work to break free of your shyness, improving your life dramatically.

Like I said, I was very shy as a kid. Yet step-by-step, through countless approaches, I met more people and I started discovering the patterns of interaction—that there is a natural sequence of events that takes place in every such interaction. The more I learned about it, the more prepared I was, the less fear I had. That's what this book does: It prepares you to improve your life when you're ready, in a way and at a pace that's comfortable for and unique to you.

That brings me, full circle, to my final point of this chapter: Why do I choose Casanova for my role model, as opposed to, say, Don Juan? After all, Don Juan is famous (or notorious, depending on your perspective) for having slept with thousands of women, while Casanova only had 122, by his own account. But the reason that I favor Casanova and he is still today so popular—his very name is now synonymous with seduction—is because he was picky. Casanova, on the one hand, had really nice, classy women. The fictional character Don Juan, on the other hand, was more like the literary equivalent of Wilt Chamberlain—he basically screwed anything that moved. So given the choice, I've had fewer women than I could have had because I say no far more than I say yes.

On that note, turn the page and join me as we begin on your journey to pickup mastery.

2.

THE ULTIMATE PURPOSE OF LIFE

Without survival, there is no life.

All life on earth has been designed by evolutionary processes to replicate. This is nature's long-established **engine of survival.**

THE PENULTIMATE PURPOSE OF LIFE

While your primary purpose in life is to survive, your secondary purpose is to replicate. In humans, natural selection has favored a method of replication that allows for genetic variation. Just as a superior basketball player limited by lousy teammates must escape and join a better team in order to win, so, too, must a superior gene *escape*

from its inferior *gene-mates* and be given a chance to join a better *genetic team* for its continued survival. This method of *escape* is called crossbreeding.

Over successive generations, crossbreeding ultimately has allowed you—that is, your genes—to *anticipate* changes in a dynamic physical and social environment, thereby increasing your chances for survival.

Put simply, replication is a means of *continued survival.*

YOUR PURPOSE IN THIS LIFE

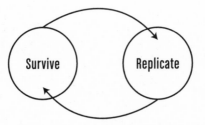

You are a biological machine. Your motives in this life are simple but not simplistic: to live and love. In order to crossbreed successfully, you must acknowledge that, in the absence of revolutionary and unforeseeable medical advancements, one day you will die.

Question:

Without calculating—just by feeling—how many DAYS do you think the average American lives?

    A. *Tens of thousands of days?*
    B. *Hundreds of thousands of days?*
    C. *Millions of days?*
    D. *Billions of days?*

DO NOT continue until you have chosen A, B, C, or D.

Answer:

(A) Tens of thousands of days.
In fact, only 28,251, to be exact.*

You have, on average, 28,251 days to live out your life. This assumes you are smart enough to *survive* this long. Even if you live to be one hundred, that still only gives you 36,500 days.

The universe requires only two things from you: that you survive and that you replicate. Your challenge is to replicate before your limited life span naturally expires. The most logical course of action is simple:

- ✦ Acknowledge the need to accelerate the learning curve through disciplined focus.
- ✦ Obtain useful S-and-R strategies from others.
- ✦ Through practice and training, internalize this knowledge into your automated motor response for practical real-life application.

There are many ways to help you survive. One such way is to learn the martial arts. There are also many ways to help you replicate. One such way is to learn the Venusian arts.

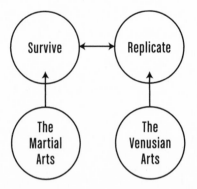

---

* According to the National Center for Health Statistics in 2002.

The martial arts (the Art of War) are really the arts of self-defense. They are disciplines that aid *survival.*

> ✦ **MARTIAL:**
> *[Roman god of war] Of, relating to, or suited for war or a warrior*

The Venusian arts (the Art of Love) are the arts of picking up a woman you had not previously met and successfully beginning an intimate relationship with her. This is a discipline that aids *replication.*

> ✦ **VENUSIAN:**
> *Of or relating to the planet Venus, Roman goddess of love and beauty*

TRAINING FOR SURVIVAL OR REPLICATION?

There is more to winning a fight than simply punching first, and as any martial artist knows, the naturally stronger person does not always win. Preparation and training can mean the difference between **survival** and dying.

Similarly, successfully beginning a sexual relationship requires more than just good looks. Expertly executing a good game plan that arrays all necessary variables can mean the difference between successful **replication** and having your genes unapologetically weeded out of existence.

Although opposites, the martial and Venusian arts also possess many parallels:

- ✦ Both are disciplines in dynamic social interaction, and each is, for many, a way of life.
- ✦ Both rank proficiency, through colored belts for martial artists and colored charms hung on black cords for Venusian artists.
- ✦ Each also embodies a comprehensive mental component that is expressed through physicality.

The difference is that in the martial arts social interactions are sometimes best avoided. In the Venusian arts social interaction is a prerequisite to success.

Bruce Lee's fighting style Jeet Kune Do (Way of the Intercepting Fist) is a martial art. Similarly, Mystery's MM (the Mystery Method) is a Venusian art. Bruce Lee was a legendary martial artist, perhaps the greatest of all time. Yet his life's accomplishments suggest that for him, martial arts were only half of a greater whole. It's no secret Bruce also identified with other—socially rewarding—pursuits. He was a great actor and celebrity. He was a great leader and a great role model. He was a great teacher and a great father. He was defined as more than *a martial artist*. Defined by his more social roles, he was also *a Venusian artist . . .* and a good one.

DYNAMIC SOCIAL HOMEOSTASIS

All social animals, including people, live under constant pressure from two competing interests: protecting themselves *from* others and aligning themselves *with* others. When these two interests are balanced, the result is **dynamic social homeostasis.**

Replication could not occur on any scale if men and women overprotected themselves by never leaving home. At the same time, the Venusian arts would be unnecessary if men and women were completely naive and didn't worry about protecting themselves and their loved ones from new encounters. If you have too much or too little of either protection *or* alignment, you have failed to achieve dynamic social homeostasis, lessening your probability of surviving or replicating successfully.

What drives us toward dynamic social homeostasis in the first place? Three millimeters of convoluted gray matter, separating us from the apes, called the cerebral cortex. That is, through natural selection, evolution has *designed* your mind to emote powerfully and in ways that contribute directly to both survival and replication. "Emote" refers specifically to a behavioral concept; that is, your *emotions* carry out an evolutionarily validated strategy that aims to keep you striving toward this perfectly balanced state.

This becomes more important all the time because of the population explosion. Today we have to be more socially intelligent than ever before in human history. After all, human beings' greatest danger on the planet is no longer predators devouring them or a raging waterfall drowning them—it's other human beings beating them in the game of life. Our interactions with other people are as much a part of our environment as rivers and trees, and we've adapted and evolved to navigate these uncharted waters with increasingly sophisticated emotional circuitry. The job of these circuits is to push us back toward homeostasis when we drift too far from it.

A BIOLOGICAL MACHINE

As noted earlier, you are a biological machine. However, while unimaginably sophisticated and complicated, you are nonetheless an out-of-date model.

Put simply, nature has not *designed* you for the world in which you live.

Certainly our *physical* environment has changed relatively little over the past one hundred thousand years or so. Then, as now, the sky was blue, trees were green, sometimes the sun shone, sometimes the clouds rained. It is our *social* environment that has changed dramatically. Namely, we live in the midst of an unprecedented population explosion fueled by innovations in technology and medical science. As a result, never in Earth's history have so many similarly designed human machines existed at any one time.

As of this writing, an estimated 6.45 billion people live on our planet.* Experts predict that in only thirty years that figure will be closer to 10 billion.

When I was born in the 1970s, 4 billion people occupied the planet. In the mid-1700s, around the time of Casanova, there were only 750 million people; ten thousand years ago, only 30 million, less than Cal-

---

* According to the population division of the U.S. Census Bureau in 2004.

ifornia's current population. Looking further back in time, to around 120,000 years ago, there were only ten to forty thousand humans living on the planet.

Our struggle for survival and replication occurs within a dynamically changing social environment. Ever since humankind came into existence, we have been faced with the challenge of trying to survive and replicate amid an ever-growing number of human competitors.

Physical adaptations always lag behind environmental ones. First, the physical world changes; only then, slowly, does the human body adapt. We're evolved biologically to live in small groups of hunters and gatherers, yet many of us occupy cities teeming with millions. We've been able to do this because the development of "culture" (tools, language, etc.) has enabled humans to circumvent physical limitations in myriad ways that other animals cannot.

Consider the new challenges this presents to the human body, given that nature hasn't yet had the chance to recalibrate it—including the behavioral and emotional circuitry that is key for successful replication—for this new social environment.

You are, in fact, best adapted for prehistory, forty and sixty thousand years before the present population explosion, when *Homo sapiens* diverged once and for all from other primates. You are, in other words, a prisoner in time, designed for social structures long since extinct. You may eat at Burger King, fly in airplanes, and surf the Internet, but your genetic coding differs little from that of men who lived in caves and chased dinner holding spears and wearing loincloths.

S-AND-R VALUE

You are not the only human being who is designed to survive and replicate. In fact, everyone, women included, harbors the same basic instincts. People form social alignments with one another whenever such arrangements benefit or enhance each person's chances of survival and replication. Our attraction circuits are in fact genetic "judges" of the S-and-R value of others.

All humans possess a built-in motivation to stay away from people with low or negative social value. In contrast, we may vastly improve our chances for survival and replication if we proactively seek out and form partnerships, both sexual and nonsexual, with those who offer us a high S-and-R value. These people would include the rich friend who loaned you money when you were broke, the socially connected acquaintance who got you into the party, the buddy who protected you from that bully, the physically fit woman who had sex with you, even the mentor who taught you how to pick her up. All are said to have high social value, and we are hardwired to seek alignment with them.

We may draw value from other people by influencing them to help us, but in a fair exchange, we must work to improve their chances as well. If one were to take too much from the other person, he or she would lower the other's chances of survival and replication.

When a woman agrees to align with you sexually, she is agreeing to trade her replication value for your value. Such fair arrangements may last many years.

APPROACH ANXIETY

Have you ever asked yourself why it is that you get an overwhelming urge to mate with a woman possessing high replication value—and then almost simultaneously get an equally overwhelming urge to run away? This behavior seems illogical and counterproductive; after all, rejection causes little harm. Emotionally, however, rejection can be a brutal experience, lasting hours, weeks, and even months. This fear is known as **approach anxiety.**

Fear of Reprisal
One reason for approach anxiety is the possibility that a woman may already be taken and the implications this might have for one's well-being, even survival. In tribal times, if you hit on a woman and her man happened to possess loyal friends, he could convince several

of them to each drop a big rock on your head and leave you for predators in an effort to protect his investment.

Fear of Rejection

To fully understand approach anxiety, we must first look at the ancient environment for which we are designed. In tribal times, only a
small, select number of women in any given tribe were available for
breeding. If a man approached one of them and then accidentally said
or did something that conveyed a low or negative S-and-R value, he
faced the real possibility of all the other women in the tribe eventually
hearing about it. No longer believed to possess S-and-R value for *any*
woman, the man would simply never mate, weeding his genes out of
existence. This real-world social pressure extends so far back in humanity's past that we have evolved acutely sensitive mental mechanisms to protect ourselves from losing social value in this way.

Even though our logical minds tell us that laws protect us from
reprisal and rejection in our modern social order, many great pickup
artists agree: The fear of a cold approach never goes away. It's hardwired into your brain. Confidence is not the objective. Competence is.

MASLOW'S HIERARCHY OF NEEDS

Bound by the human condition, you have a **hierarchy of needs** and
everything you do results directly or indirectly from emotions that *demand* that you (and your target) meet them.

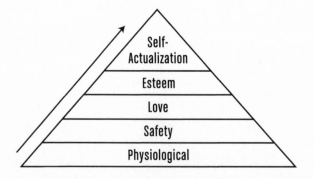

Established by noted psychologist Abraham Maslow, this theory says that human beings are motivated by unsatisfied needs. What's more, he says, in a hierarchical fashion certain lower needs *must* be satisfied before higher needs can be.

Think about it: If you were choking on a sandwich right now, your need for oxygen would be stronger than your need for love. If nobody loved you it would suck, without question, but you wouldn't die instantly.

- **Physiological:** The most basic needs, such as air, water, food, warmth, sleep, and sex.
- **Safety:** Establishing stability and consistency in a chaotic world. In modern times this is mostly psychological.
- **Love:** The need to belong. People desire to be loved and accepted by others.
- **Esteem:** This internally generated feeling usually results from achieving competence in or mastering a task. Attention, recognition, and social status come from others.
- **Self-Actualization:** We desire to become everything that we are capable of becoming. People who have met all of their lower needs can then maximize their potential.

VITAL AREAS OF FOCUS

To meet each of your needs and satisfy your highly evolved emotional system—thereby fulfilling your purpose in life—you must focus on three vital areas. Every time you have marked success in any of these areas, your mind rewards you with a feeling of *happiness.*

This simple model is as old as the Kabbalah, and success in the three areas of *health*, *wealth*, and *love* will ensure your survival and replication.

- ✦ **Health:** Refers to both the body *and* the mind. You need a proven method or *game plan* to maintain your health.
- ✦ **Wealth:** Helps you to maintain your health and your relationships. You need a roof over your head, clothes on your back, and food in your stomach. Additional creature comforts assist in your survival and replication. An apartment may keep you warm and dry but also provides a private location for sex. A vehicle not only enables you to make money but also improves your romantic options by extending your effective range. You need a proven wealth-building game plan to achieve financial independence and to *fund your game* for romantic pursuits. It also costs money to purchase a gym membership, dress well, and socialize at a nightclub or restaurant.
- ✦ **Love:** Refers mainly to your romantic relationships but may also extend to friends, family members, and business relationships with associates. If you want to have successful loving relationships, you must study them.

Any area can be *maintained, improved,* or *neglected.* Your success in each of the three areas can be rated on an ascending scale from 1 to 10. Rate a 10 in any area and you need only maintain it. Anything below a 10 and you must devise a way to improve your success in that area. If you neglect an area too long and your rating falls too low, the quality of your *entire* life will decline.

Each **vital area of focus** is connected to the other two areas in countless ways.

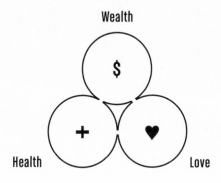

Wealth

Health Love

Health, wealth, and *love* share an intimate relationship with one another. Success in any one vital area will positively affect the other two. In fact, to improve in a certain area, sometimes you must first focus on and improve another area. For example, you can increase your success in love by maintaining or improving your wealth as well as your health. People who are healthy, fit, and energetic in social situations project a higher replication value and thus are more likely to connect with and attract those around them.

At the same time, neglecting to maintain any one area will negatively affect the other two. When you neglect any area for too long, the ill effects can quickly infect a second area, which in turn can infect a third, and so on. This runaway chain reaction is called **spiraling** and, if left unbridled, can undermine your life's prime directives. Rationing your time equally among all three vital areas is crucial in preventing a downward spiral that can lead to a **great collapse** (sickness, poverty, and loneliness). I've seen people all around the world whose lives have spiraled into dismay.

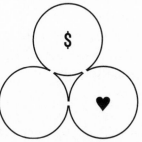

HEALTH NEGLECT: If you have *wealth* and success in *love* (relationships) but are lacking in *health* (mental or physical), eventually you'll have decreased success in the areas of wealth (through lowered productivity and energy levels)

and relationships. People who don't respect themselves are seldom respected by others. Unhealthy people are simply not attractive.

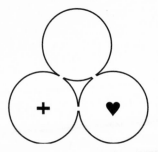

WEALTH NEGLECT: If you have *health* and relationship success (*love*) but fail in the area of *wealth*, eventually you won't have the resources to sustain *love* (unable to pay cover charges for instance) or the means to maintain *health* (proper food, healthy physical environment, and exercise equipment). A big bed in your own condo not only allows you to sleep better than on your parents' couch (*health*) but also rewards you with a place to bring a woman (*love*).

LOVE (RELATIONSHIPS) NEGLECT: If you are *healthy* and *wealthy* but don't have success in your relationships, this failure will make you feel lonely and compromise your self-esteem (*mental health*). It will also undermine your wealth-building plans. In business, you'll have a tough time making new contacts, networking, and

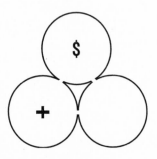

appearing "together," which will affect your *wealth*-building potential.

You must maintain or improve all three vital areas of your life while keeping them in balance. If you aren't getting the results you want while practicing your game, it's time to examine your social life in general, your health and fitness, and your career.

REVIEW

+ The ultimate purpose of life is survival.
+ The penultimate purpose of life is replication. Someday you

will die. Before that time comes, you must pass on your genes.

* The average person lives for just 28,251 days. The logical course of action is to determine the most effective way to survive and replicate and practice this until it becomes an automatic response.

* The martial arts consist of practiced routines that, once internalized, improve your survival chances. The Venusian arts consist of practiced routines and best practices that, once internalized, improve your replication chances.

* **Dynamic social homeostasis** is the balance between the drive to protect ourselves from others and the drive to align ourselves with others.

* Our emotional circuitry is designed to best suit our S-and-R based on an ancient environment and tribal social order that once existed tens of thousands of years ago. People make sexual decisions largely based on this emotional circuitry.

* People tend to form **social alignments** with one another, wherever such alignments most benefit their chances of survival and replication.

* Men take a larger risk than women when first approaching. In ancient times this posed a legitimate safety concern, and thus men still experience **approach anxiety.**

* Women will find a man more attractive if he has already been **preselected** by other women.

* Bound by the human condition, everyone has a hierarchy of needs that must be met, including physiological needs, safety needs, social needs, and so on. Our emotions are designed to motivate us to get these needs met.

* We most focus on three vital areas of life: health, wealth, and love. Deficiencies in any one of these categories will create problems in the other two.

3.

REWIRING HER
ATTRACTION CIRCUITRY

CREATURES OF SENTIMENT

Logic and reason can be used to determine a course of action, but often men and women alike are motivated more persuasively by their emotions. Often we simply use our intellects to rationalize those emotional actions after the fact.

To women, emotions are much more profound and encompassing than they are even to men. Because a woman's attraction circuitry is calibrated less to a man's physical characteristics than to his social, and hence survival, value, her emotions are at the center of her thoughts and actions. In fact, when a woman explains something, she will often use emotions as legitimate reasons unto themselves. Just "feeling" something to be true is reason enough. Women simply have more acute social triggers differentially designed into their behavior system due to their need to assess a potential mate's social value. As a result . . .

Don't Try to Convince Her

Don't bother trying to convince her, argue with her, or engage her in any other way on a purely logical level. Logic should never be used as a motivator in the field, because what a woman thinks she likes, or says she likes, is not necessarily what she responds to in reality.

Stimulate Her Emotions

The Venusian artist uses **emotional stimulation** instead of rational discourse. As long as it *feels* right, your romantic interest will invent her own reasons for what is happening. In other words, a woman will come up with a thousand reasons that she shouldn't have sex with you—but she will also come up with a thousand reasons for why she did.

Never Be Apathetic

A woman knows how susceptible to persuasion she becomes in an excited emotional state. Often her safeguard is to avoid the risk of becoming emotionally engaged in an interaction where she doesn't feel trust or safety, or where the man gaming her doesn't adequately demonstrate a high S-and-R value. After all, allowing a man with low value to influence her emotionally is counterproductive. So engaging a woman on an emotional level, even if it involves a "bad" emotion such as frustration or jealousy, is preferable to not engaging her at all.

Instead of only trying to give her "good" emotions while avoiding "bad" ones, stimulate her with a range of feelings including curiosity, fascination, connection, indignation, validation, laughter, embarrassment, happiness, sadness, and fear of value loss. The more she is stimulated, the more compelling the experience will be for her. The entire A2 phase of the Mystery Method, detailed in chapter 6, is dedicated to the technique for this.

INTUITION TRUMPS ANALYSIS

If a woman wants to determine if you are being real with her, she won't use logic to analyze what you said for inconsistencies. Instead, she'll observe

Female Intuition at Work

Women often look for the "real meaning" behind what you say. For example, if you tell a story about your "friend," a woman may assume that you are actually talking about yourself. Women possess what is called dynamic social intuition.

your *actions* to see if *you* appear congruent with what you are saying. Women follow their intuition over analysis.

PEACOCK THEORY

Just as a long, cumbersome appendage on the end of a male bird is costly evidence of its survival abilities (something peahens want in their offspring), a person is said to **peacock** when he or she wears attention-getting clothes. This prompts others to interact with him or her. If you "peacock," girls will look at you more often, while lower-value guys will make sniggering comments. This means that there will be more social pressure on you than you would normally experience, which can be used to your advantage.

You demonstrate higher value when people perceive that you're accustomed to this social pressure and otherwise unaffected by it. Even though you're wearing nonconformist clothing, you can still survive in this world! Women will think, *Wow, despite that "tail," he's still here; he's still alive!* They will perceive this as social dominance.

The key is that people must see your personality as **congruent** with your "peacocked" image. A man with a top hat and a feather boa, a woman on each arm, surrounded by laughing friends, looks like *the man.* Everyone in the room will notice him, and women will whisper to one another and want to be introduced to him. But the same man in those same clothes sitting alone in the corner will look like a social reject.

By the same token, "peacocking" should be a unique and dominant expression of higher social value; otherwise, it not only loses its desired effect but also can actually work against you in the field. One guy dressed to the nines looks like "the man"; two guys decked out that way look gay. That's why I come in like a rock star, but my other friends just wear something cool—for example, new boots, or an odd-looking chain, or a new jacket with something cool spray-painted on the back. Successful peacocking takes preparation and thought; at any time, somewhere in the world, an MM instructor is taking someone shopping to find a look that works for *him*.

You don't have to wear a top hat right out of the chute, but as my friends' example suggests, try wearing at least one item of clothing curious looking enough to get people's attention. It may be used as a **lock-in prop,** which I will discuss further in chapter 6. What's more, it will allow women to comment, for good or bad, if they wish to strike up a conversation.

For example, if you're talking to a woman and she senses the conversation winding down, she may suddenly say, "Oh, that's a cool necklace." This is her way of continuing the interaction in a perfectly reasonable way, while reserving some element of **plausible deniability,** that is, keeping the responsibility for anything that might happen "on you."

On more than one occasion I've had women walk up to me and tell me that they either loved or hated my goggles. Either way, I would reply, "No, you don't; you're attracted to me."

SOCIAL AWARENESS

You will hear women ask men, "So, what do you do?" "Where are your friends?" "Where'd you graduate?" and "Who's he?" Various kinds of social ranking are of great interest to people, especially women. These include occupation and your ranking within it, social status, reputation, and social and sexual alignments. The answers to these questions help a woman judge whether you possesses a high-enough S-and-R value for her.

Discretion Is a Virtue

When she says, "Not here," you say, "I understand."

A woman's reputation directly influences her social status. This is why women are easier to get into bed when they are on vacation—they are more likely to indulge in an adventure that they trust holds no social consequences. This is also why women are appreciative of men who understand and practice **discretion.**

A Venusian artist will never brag publicly about his sexual conquests unless doing so (with her permission) legitimately raises her social status. If you brag, not only will it eventually get back to her, but also any other woman who hears it will be on notice that sexual relations with you carry social consequences. So, for example, when you obtain a phone number from a woman, don't walk straight to your friends and high-five them for all to see.

The Anti-Slut Defense

The word "slut" is a weapon women use against other women in an attempt to lower their competitors' perceived social value.

Women have a powerful interruption mechanism known to pickup artists as the **anti-slut defense (ASD).** Not only do women prefer to avoid having others *perceive* them as sluts, but they also want to avoid the discomfort of *feeling* like a slut. So a woman's highly calibrated ASD circuit acts as an interrupt mechanism to help her avoid this fate.

Be aware of others in proximity, as their presence alone may influence the behavior of the woman you are trying to kiss.

Plausible Deniability

A woman will rarely do anything during the pickup that makes her feel responsible for what may happen between the two of you. To whatever degree she feels responsible, her anti-slut defense will be activated.

Thus she has a need for **plausible deniability.** For example, if you were to say to her, "Hey, let's go back to my place and have sex," she would have to say no, even though she wanted to say yes, *because saying yes would make her responsible for what is happening*—which she can never be.

But if instead you were to say, "Hey, let's stop by my place on the way to that party; I have to show you my tropical fish," now she has an excuse and plausible deniability to stop by your place and then—oopsie!—have sex with you. *"One thing led to another . . ."*

This is why serendipity is so romantic. After all, if it was *meant to be,* then how can it be her fault? Who is she to deny Fate?

Act with Moxie

"Moxie" means "inventive courage." The Venusian artist must always be leading the interaction. He has no choice. Women seldom take responsibility for what is happening.

For example, it is necessary to keep things interesting during the opening phase of the game. If you don't work to steer the conversation onto interesting topics, the woman may accidentally raise her own boring topics—and then she'll feel bored and blame it on you.

It may not seem fair that we men are responsible for leading the conversation, but if we don't, then we may lose the girl. If she feels bored around you but excited around another guy, why should she waste her time on you?

Make things happen. Take responsibility for your shared experience with her. It's your job to foster each shared moment and lead her from one to the next with moxie, whether it's moving from phase to phase, meeting the objectives of each phase, escalating, venue changing, or something else. (You will learn how to do this step-by-step in the very next chapter.) If she's boring and bored, it's your fault.

Persistence

This is another way to relieve her of any responsibility for what is happening. Of course, don't confuse persistence with begging, arguing, or being pushy, needy, or creepy. All it means is *don't give up too easily.* Girls may test you to find out how easily you throw in the towel—they want to gauge your self-confidence. Just assume that she is giving a little token resistance, and continue. If she didn't resist at least a little bit, she would feel like a slut—and that's not going to happen. And if *you* can't take her crap, how in the world are you going to protect her from *other* people's crap?

This can be tricky—an overly aggressive man might misinterpret *all* resistance as being merely token and could eventually find himself facing a rape charge. However, a man who isn't persistent enough will acquiesce every time a woman resists, when in many cases she was secretly hoping that he could be a little more forceful.

CONGRUENCE TESTS

A woman's number-one emotional priority is safety and security. Above all, she wants a man who makes her feel safe and protected.

It would be most convenient if she could simply ask each man whether he would be able to adequately support and protect her and her offspring. But, of course, he would then lie in order to obtain sex. So she must test.

It's important to remember that often she is not deliberately testing you. It's not necessarily something that she is consciously aware of. She just gets a feeling to behave a certain way, and so she does. Depending on how you react, she feels either *more* or *less* attracted as a result. This is known as a **congruence test.**

If she views you as a contender, then she *will* test you. A woman often won't even bother to test a low-value male; instead, she will just become nonresponsive and then leave as soon as possible. Thus a test can be considered an **indicator of interest** of sorts.

Congruence tests are a double-edged sword: If you respond the right way, she will be noticeably more attracted to you after the test. But if you fail, then she will be noticeably less attracted. (Chapter 7 explains how to pass her tests.)

Appeasement Is Futile

Women will keep pushing and testing until they find all your boundaries. When a woman pushes and feels that resistance, it allows her to *feel secure* with you. This is what she's looking for. But if she doesn't feel that resistance, then she will keep pushing until she walks all over you and then seeks challenge elsewhere.

Of course a woman will be unable to respect a man if she can walk all over him. It'll be mildly disappointing to her, but she'll also feel reassured about her feminine power—which feels good—and she may even reward his submission with positive reinforcement. Good doggy.

The moral is, just because you compliment a girl doesn't mean it will bring you any closer to sex. A girl may enjoy the ego boost when men catcall at her—but she will rarely, if ever, have sex with those men.

INVESTMENT

Although you may be an attractive guy with relatively high S-and-R value, another guy just like you could easily come along tomorrow.

In the moment, when she is intoxicated with the emotions of flirting with you and she gives you her phone number, she may have every intention of following up with you in the future. But once you are separated, memories slowly fade and new flirtations arise.

So it's not enough for her to be attracted to you. She must become **invested** in her interaction with you before parting. The more invested she is in her interaction with you, the more motivated she will be to get a return on that investment.

In other words, the more time she spends with you, the more money she spends on you, the more effort she exerts to get your attention or validation, the more she is emotionally and physically engaged with you, the more likely you will begin a sexual relationship with her.

What are some forms of investment?

+ **Emotional investment:** Women are reluctant to allow themselves to become emotionally vulnerable around men of dubious intent or low S-and-R value. A woman knows that once she gets emotional, it becomes much more difficult to extract herself from the situation.
+ **Physical investment:** Kissing is a bigger investment than walking arm in arm. Sex is a bigger investment than kissing.
+ **Time:** The more time you spend together, the more invested

she becomes. It takes an average of four to ten hours to develop enough familiarity for sex.

✦ **Effort:** Is she chasing? People don't value that which comes too easily. The more effort she puts in, the more invested she has become.

✦ **Money:** Did you buy her a drink, or did she buy one for you?

Many of the tactics in the game are not designed to attract her but rather to use that attraction as bait in order to get her more *invested* in her interaction with you. (See chapter 7 for these tactics.)

DISCOMFORT AND CONFRONTATION

Women tend to avoid discomfort and confrontation. This may seem like common sense, but these points are *critical* to achieving success in the game:

✦ **Have a positive, open attitude.** Don't be judgmental or jealous.

✦ **Don't act as if things are a *big deal*.** They aren't.

✦ **Don't complain or be emotionally punishing.** If you call her on her shit while talking on the phone, she will just avoid talking to you on the phone. Instead of being the whiny or emotionally abusive boyfriend whenever she pulls a fast one, be the guy who has plenty of relationship options.

✦ **If she flakes on you, don't confront her about it next time you see her.** Are you the guy who sat around and got upset? Or are you the guy who called over another girl and then forgot all about it?

FUN AND STIMULATION

Just as she tends to avoid discomfort, so she is also attracted to fun and stimulation (once her safety has been secured, of course.) Attractive women are often found on boats or dance floors, at parties or in nice cars, around bad boys and rich men. These scenarios are much more compelling than just hanging with a *nice guy*. To avoid that fate:

- **Be a fun and playful person.** This is preferable to appearing *tough* or *"too deep."*
- **Be challenging to women.** They value challenge.
- **Be slightly unpredictable.** Familiarity breeds contempt.
- **Embrace your passions** and be involved in activities. (See chapter 8 for more information on building a strong identity.)
- **Develop your social circle.** Invest time and energy in cultivating it.

Keeping a woman around is an active process. After you win her over, you can't just put her in a box and pull her out like a toy when you feel like playing with it. She needs adequate love and attention, stimulation, a firm hand, and several trillion other things. She will never be completely content, but it *is* possible to keep her coming back for more. Your objective isn't to have sex with her. It's to allow her to *fall in love* with you.

WOMEN UNDERSTAND SOCIAL DYNAMICS

Women are wonderful creatures, but they are not angels of purity and morality. They are human just like the rest of us. In the field, you often may notice women lying or using other manipulation. They may act jealous, try to make *you* jealous, use their sexuality to gain power, lie about their age or give you a wrong number, stir up trouble, or, without hesitation, ditch you for something shinier—someone with higher status, more testosterone, better cocaine.

And as empathetic as women are deemed to be, they will not necessarily later wallow in pathos with a solitary tear on her cheek, full of regret for ditching you. Don't take it personally; you just didn't convey enough S-and-R value for them by the time they had to choose whether to see you again. It's just part of the game. Matador, one of my top instructors, was telling me about a student he had who came to his three-day MM workshop. On the first night, the woman in whom he was interested blew him off. The second night, he ran into her again, and as he was armed with more advanced skills he'd learned that very day, she soon was begging him to take her phone number. Same guy. Same girl. Different result.

RATING A WOMAN'S APPEARANCE

Men seek more replication value than survival value from women, and women seek more survival value than replication value from men. In fact, the women of health-and-beauty-conscious America, though perhaps disgruntled by the true nature of their humanity, are well aware that their social value can be rated largely on their looks.

Pickup artists have employed a low-threshold decimal-rating system to score a woman's appearance from 6 to 10, with a 6 being an OK-looking girl and a 10 being supermodel hot. We do not rate below a 6. Women may understandably feel it sexist to be privately referred to by a number, such as a 7 or a 9, but sexism is prejudice or discrimination based on sex, not perceived survival and replication value. This is different.

Women, along with men, must accept the fundamental reality of humanity: Judiciously assessing another's social value directly influences whether their offspring will possess high S-and-R value.

Women of different ratings respond differently, so pickup artists need to assess a woman's objective social value and calibrate their game accordingly. Furthermore, men *and* women will also respond differently to others based on the perception of their relative difference in social status. Seeking rapport, for instance, is often an easy way to open a conversation with a set of 7s but will only get you blown out with a set of 10s. Being cocky and challenging, which 9s and 10s absolutely love, will often cause a 6 or a 7 to react in a nasty way.

The Mystery Method, with its emphasis on raising one's long-term social value, is geared toward attracting 10s. In fact, you may have to tone down aspects of your game if you are dealing with a less-than-beautiful woman, or she might reject you to protect her own ego. It's easier for her to shoot down a guy for an immediate ego boost than to risk being rejected by one whom she didn't feel qualified for in the first place.

CAT THEORY

Why do you suppose we only feel compelled to chase the ones who run away?

—VICOMTE DE VALMONT,
Les Liaisons Dangereuses

Cats don't take orders, but they can be tempted to chase. If you tie a feather to the end of a string *and use it properly,* you can get a cat to perform acrobatics. But isn't it interesting that if you put the feather down in front of the cat, it will turn up its nose?

Cats are always curious, especially about shiny new things such as a ball on a rubber cord, catnip, treats, the feather on a string, et cetera. They can be easily distracted, but once they are invested in trying to catch something, it can become their single-minded focus.

There is a lot to learn from cats. If you push cats off of you, they jump back into your lap. If you want to hold them, then they want you to put them down. If they are feeling nasty, they might bite or scratch. Cats crave attention and get jealous of other cats. Sometimes cats will just rub against you and purr with contentment—you can really tell when a cat likes someone.

As the Venusian artist proceeds with a pickup, he keeps validation and attention just *slightly* out of the target's reach. If he is too easily acquired, then a woman will quickly grow bored and lose interest. But likewise if he is completely unattainable, then she will also lose interest and give up.

Therefore, keep the bait just barely out of her reach and then continually entice her in small increments.

BOYFRIENDS

Nine times out of ten, when a woman says, "I have a boyfriend," what this translates to is, "You just telegraphed too much interest."

It has nothing to do with whether she actually has a boyfriend. In fact, if she is attracted to you, she will often deliberately hide the boyfriend from you until after you have had sex with her.

Whether she mentions him or not in no way proves that he actually exists—only that she had a motive to mention him.

Some Reasons That a Woman Might Say She Has a Boyfriend

1. Though she doesn't have a boyfriend, she's not attracted to you or you miscalibrated your escalation.
2. She *does* have a boyfriend and, given her current options, she has chosen to stick with that relationship.
3. She *does* have a boyfriend and *is* willing to sleep with you but wants to make sure that you understand her situation first. She wants *discretion* and *understanding*. And though she might be available to you for sex, she's *not* immediately available for any more of a commitment.
4. She *does* have a boyfriend and she *is* willing to cheat on him (they often are if your game is tight), but she doesn't want to feel guilty about it. This is her **rationalization** process at work. As long as she mentions the boyfriend *before* sleeping with you, she can rationalize to herself that it was *your fault*. Sure, she might regret it later, but that won't necessarily stop her from cheating.
5. She *doesn't* have a boyfriend and she *is* attracted to you; she just doesn't want to look like a loser who can't get a man. Most hot women have **orbiters** anyway: nice guys who pose as their friends but secretly want to sleep with them. Since the word "boyfriend" can have so many different meanings, she is thinking of one of her orbiters as a "place keeper."

The bottom line is, don't ask about her boyfriend and don't appear fazed if she mentions him. He may not even exist. Just take it as an instance of a lack of interest caused by you telegraphing too much interest far too soon.

REVIEW

+ Emotions are circuits in the brain that judge value and create motivation. They are designed to keep you alive and to replicate your genes.
+ People are likely to act based on their emotions and then **backward-rationalize.** Because women have highly developed emotional circuits, they are especially susceptible to this.
+ People seek alignments and pair bonds based on S-and-R value.
+ Women take a much larger risk, evolutionarily speaking, when they have sex. Sex is also a much larger investment for them than it is for men. For this reason, women have emotional circuitry designed to take this into account. For example, women tend to experience much more anxiety just prior to sex with a new lover.
+ Don't bother trying to convince a woman, argue with her, or otherwise engage her on a logical level.
+ What a woman likes, or says she likes, is not necessarily what she responds to emotionally (and thus sexually.)
+ If a woman remains **nonresponsive,** that means she is deliberately cutting you off from gaming her. A woman will not allow herself to become emotionally vulnerable around you if you haven't demonstrated enough value or if she doesn't feel safe enough.
+ **Peacocking** is the use of attention-getting clothes to amplify your responses in the field. Try wearing at least one item that is cool and attracts attention.

+ A woman's **reputation** is often very important to her, and thus she is much more likely to indulge sexually when she trusts that there will be no **social consequences.**

+ All women have a powerful interruption mechanism known as **anti-slut defense,** or **ASD.** When you play solid game, you will be able to escalate smoothly without triggering a woman's anti-slut defense.

+ A woman often won't do anything that makes her feel responsible for the escalation—she needs **plausible deniability.** The Venusian artist must take responsibility to make things happen and act with **moxie.**

+ A woman may use **congruence tests** to provoke a reaction from you. Then her intuition tells her whether you seem congruent. She tests in this way so that she can find your boundaries, which allows her to feel secure. This behavior is instinctive and allows her to more accurately determine what sort of man you really are.

+ Most women view men as an abundant resource. Thus it's not enough to attract her—she must become **invested** in the interaction.

+ A woman will seek out fun and stimulation—and avoid confrontation and discomfort.

+ Don't act as if things are a **big deal.** Just repeat the words "no problem" in your head until you really believe it. No matter what happens, it's no big deal.

+ Part of being a man of value is pursuing your dreams, having a **strong identity,** and living a passionate life.

+ The **decimal rating scale** is used for rating women based on their appearance, from 6 to 10, an OK girl being a 6 and a supermodel being a 10.

+ As you proceed with the pickup, keep the woman just inside that window between revalidation and rejection. She must be baited to chase in **small increments,** just like a cat with a string.

+ **Don't ask about a woman's boyfriend, and don't be fazed if she mentions him.** He may not even exist.

4.

RULES AND STRUCTURE OF THE GAME

The Mystery Method comprises several aspects. First, the **M3 Model** describes the courtship process from the time a man and a woman meet until the beginning of their sexual relationship. Second, **group theory** describes the application of social dynamics and the M3 Model to groups of people found in public settings. This is important because high-caliber women are often found in this social context. Third, the Mystery Method is a *methodology* for practicing the game in the field; and fourth, it includes a set of field-proven techniques pickup artists refer to as **Venusian arts gambits** that have arisen from this methodology. These include the **neg** and the **false time constraint**, which are explained in subsequent chapters of this book.

THE GAME IS PLAYED IN THE FIELD

The Game is not played on a computer or the Internet. It's not played in a book. It's played in the real world, with real people and real situations. Only through repeated practice in the field can we develop intuition and skill. Over time, these methods become habitual. Once these methods are internalized over a few weeks of disciplined practice, it is in fact easier to keep doing them than to stop. You'll do the right thing naturally. To that end:

✦ Focus on building your skill, not on meeting your new girl-friend or "getting laid." Think about social dynamics as if you were learning a new video game.

✦ Don't obsess over a particular woman. Forget about that girl you have been pining over for the past three months. You need to train first.

✦ It is easier to attract a new woman than it is to fix things when they go wrong with your existing target. (Attraction can be generated in seconds to minutes, while sex may occur in roughly four to ten hours.)

MYSTERY'S NEWBIE MISSION

✦ Go out gaming four nights per week for four hours each night.
✦ Make an average of three approaches per hour. This schedule allows for a good twenty minutes per approach.

That adds up to twelve approaches per night—which is forty-eight per week and close to two hundred per month. (Chapter 5 covers the art of approaching.) Within a year, you will have approached more than two thousand women.

How many women have you approached in the past year?

CALIBRATION AND INTERNALIZATION

After the first week or two in the field, approaches start to become a blur. Patterns emerge over time. Formerly puzzling social behavior comes clearly into focus. Situations and reactions can be easily predicted before they occur. This powerful and acute social intuition, finely tuned from time spent in the field, is known as **calibration.**

A skilled Venusian artist will anticipate, and have a prepared response for, nearly any common social challenge. He already will have encountered this particular challenge before. He has experimented with a variety of different responses, and he has compared notes with all of his friends on the subject as well. He has found an effective answer, and he has already field-tested and mastered it.

So when the challenge arises, the answer comes forth, automatically delivered into action by his unconscious mind. In the same way that all practiced behaviors become automatic, so does the skill set of the Mystery Method. This process is known as **internalization**.

Calibration is a never-ending process for any Venusian artist, even a master. For example, as a social experiment, one time I brought a large fake cigar out to a club. For good measure, I gave several to my friends as well, and we were all out together holding these big fake cigars. This created the imagery that we were all socially aligned, and that raised our value. Being part of a group is better than being alone.

Then a woman came up to me out of the blue and said, "Why do you have a fake cigar?" I was stunned; I didn't have an answer. I replied, "Uh, I don't know . . .'cause it's fun?" I felt foolish about that response, so I thought, *There is this invisible thread hanging off of this prop. If I bring it out,* of course *someone is going to ask that question. Why didn't I know? Why didn't I prepare?* So I went home and thought of an answer. The next time I was asked that question in the field, I recited, "Because smoking *disgusts* me"—and then puffed on the fake cigar with which is funny. And I didn't get blown out of set.

Women Are More Socially Savvy Because They've Had More Practice

For a man to be in the Game, he must actively approach women. If he stops doing this, he has taken himself out of the Game. A woman cannot make this choice so easily. If she is attractive, men will approach her whether she wants them to or not. She needn't do anything but simply be there; she can't help it. For this reason, women usually have more calibration and social skill than men do, simply because they've been involved in more approaches. By the time a typical "10" is twenty-four years old, she may have been approached thousands times. A Venusian artist must be the exception.

PROCESS OVER OUTCOME

A Venusian artist goes into the field night after night primarily to *improve his calibration* and to *internalize his skill set*. You're not trying to "get this one girl" or even "get laid tonight." Rather, you *practice* with the long-term goal of having a powerful social skill set in the future, one you may confidently turn on in times of need. When you don't need it, you don't use it. When you do, you're ready.

You cannot allow the outcome of any given approach to carry much significance, at least until you reach the point—usually ten to twenty-five minutes into your set—when you decide that you legitimately prize the target. It's like playing a video game: If your man dies, just hit the reload button and play again. If the outcome of any specific approach becomes important to you, it'll have subtle, insidious effects on your game and compromise your win. You really do have to *not care*.

The one who releases himself from the emotional attachment to a desired outcome is, ironically, the one most likely to realize that outcome.

Just like surfing or scuba diving, the process of playing the Game itself is its own reward. It's fascinating to meet new people and explore their lives. If you do not enjoy exploring humanity or proactively conducting lighthearted social experiments for their own sake, you likely will not have the persistence to master the art.

After some months of practice and experience in the field, you will start to hone your game. Your skills will enable you to enjoy the alignments you've developed with beautiful women. You won't concern yourself with approach anxiety, rejection, or even outcome. You'll simply enjoy the ride.

THE STRUCTURE OF A SEXUAL RELATIONSHIP

Every long-term (sexually intimate) relationship has a beginning, middle, and ending, where . . .

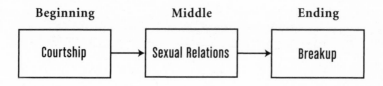

Everything you will ever learn about the Venusian arts will fall into one of these three stages.

COURTSHIP

Further, every courtship, from meeting each other to having sex, has a beginning, middle, and ending to it. You can't get to the middle until you complete the beginning, and you can't get to the ending until you first complete the beginning and the middle.

The Mystery Method focuses on only these three stages. I have named these three courtship stages . . .

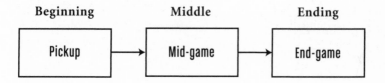

Every love story ever told and every relationship you've ever had or will ever have has a plotline that progresses through each of these three stages.

ATTRACTION

> Attract

The primary focus of the Mystery Method is not seduction but rather attraction.

✦ AT ·TRACT:

transitive senses: to cause to approach or adhere: as a: to pull to or draw toward oneself or itself < a magnet attracts iron > b: to draw by appeal to natural or excited interest, emotion, or aesthetic sense: ENTICE < attract attention >
intransitive senses: to exercise attraction
Etymology: Middle English, from Latin attractus, past participle of attrahere, from ad- + trahere to pull, draw

✦ SE ·DUCE:

1: to persuade to disobedience or disloyalty
2: to lead astray usually by persuasion or false promises
3: to carry out the physical seduction of: entice to sexual intercourse
Etymology: Middle English, from Late Latin seducere, from Latin, to lead away, from se- apart + ducere to lead
                        —*Merriam-Webster's Online Dictionary*, 10th ed.

Mystery's protégés focus on attraction first, not seduction. Ethically, they are therefore attractors, not seducers.   —MM Statement of Ethics

Attraction is not a choice.

—DAVID DEANGELO

The Secret of Attraction

A quantifiable number of fundamental attraction switches are hard wired into the sexual selection mechanism of every man and woman on earth.

In the same way that we men automatically feel an overwhelming attraction toward any *Sports Illustrated* swimsuit model because she turns on all our attraction switches, women can be made to feel exactly the same way toward *us* if we only devise a clever method for systematically turning on all *their* attraction switches.

Certain switches turn on in the presence of legitimate replication value. At the same time, switches can also turn off in the presence of indicators suggesting negative replication value. It's Darwinian: Mating with a young, fit girl rather than a menopausal woman will improve your genes' chances of successful replication.

Our switches are wired to respond to qualities such as specific hip-to-waist ratios, breast shape and size, facial and body symmetry, and other indicators of youth and health. For that reason, if a woman possesses and can demonstrate a certain quality that one of your sexual selection switches is programmed to respond to, you'll feel immediate attraction for her, without the need to even think about it. **In fact, you won't even have a choice in the matter.**

It is interesting to note that . . .

+ the majority of a man's attraction switches are set to respond to a woman's replication value; only a minority respond to her survival value.
+ only a minority of a woman's switches are set to respond to a man's replication value, while the majority respond to his survival value.

Even if a woman's breasts are fake, you will feel greater attraction for her than if she were small breasted. So many women wouldn't go to such extremes (plastic surgery, etc.) if the results didn't in fact work to trigger attraction. Our attraction circuits are calibrated to feel subtle indicators to a woman's replication value.

So what qualities in a man are a woman's attraction switches set to respond to, and how do we systematically turn them on in rapid succession and in a practical manner in the field?

Previously I have discussed basic qualities such as health and fitness, being comfortable and smiling, and so on. Now let's examine an attraction switch that is an order of magnitude greater in power. . . .

Preselection

This attraction switch exists not only in the sexual selection mechanisms of people but also in many animals. A male grouse (a type of bird) will be hard-pressed to attract a female if he is alone. Place a stuffed female grouse beside him, and other females will soon enter his territory and mate with him.

Similarly, if a woman considers a man to be sexually attractive to other women, she may instantly feel an attraction toward him. Stand by yourself at the bar and you will not appear nearly as attractive as you would if you had women hanging off both arms.

Demonstrating that you have women interested in you, in this direct manner, is only one of many ways to trigger the same sexual selection switch. There are other ways. You can also wear women's perfume. When a woman asks what you are wearing say, "Nothing." Smell your collar and then, as if remembering, say, "Ah," and smile to yourself.

Another way to flip her preselection switch is to have a lipstick kiss on your cheek. In the exact same way you feel greater attraction for a woman if she has an appealing hip-to-waist ratio, a woman will feel toward you because of that all-important lipstick kiss.

There are a good many more ways to flip the preselection switch, and there are many more switches to be flipped. The secret of attraction is to know what these switches are and then endeavor to systematically switch all of them on! There is no quicker or more powerful attraction.

Chapters 6 and 7 examine the subject of attraction in depth, as well as the various tactics for generating and using it.

THE M3 MODEL

Only after you attract can seduction take place. However, before a woman who is attracted to you will be seduced, there is one additional crucial stage: *You must build comfort.* (Chapters 8 and 9 describe the comfort and seduction phases of the Mystery Method.)

We now have the main focus for each stage in M3:

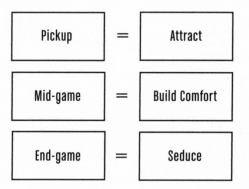

Seduction Is Mutual

If you can build enough comfort with a woman for her to be alone in a room with you during the mid-game stage, then she will readily agree to have sex with you in the end-game stage. **In fact, she may very well try to seduce you.**

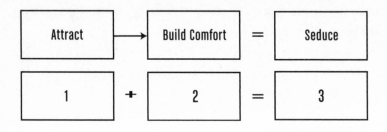

Therefore, if you work to structure a convenient opportunity for her to seduce you, there will otherwise be little reason to focus directly on seduction itself.

Unfortunately, none of this is possible without attraction. She will certainly not accept your comfort-building efforts if there's no attraction—especially if she has been socialized by being hit on by an endless line of nice guys. Be warned: If you seek comfort prematurely, it will only make you less attractive to her. Or worse, you'll get stuck in the **friendship zone.** (More on that momentarily.)

To recap, the three main objectives in the Mystery Method are:

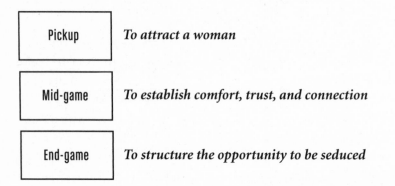

THE ELUSIVE OBVIOUS

Illustrated thus simply, the linear relationship between attraction, comfort, and seduction seems intuitive and self-evident. Yet pickup

artists the world over have repeatedly struggled with problems that
arise from improper M3 sequencing.

THE FOUR M3 SEQUENCING MISTAKES

1. **Seduction first**—*to start at the end.*
2. **Comfort first**—*to start in the middle.*
3. **Attraction but no comfort**—*to start at the beginning but skip the middle and go straight to the end.*
4. **Attraction and comfort only**—*to start at the beginning but get stuck in the middle.*

SEQUENCING MISTAKE #1: TO START AT THE END

Ending

```
┌─────────────────┐
│                 │
│     Seduce      │
│                 │
└─────────────────┘
```

The Seducer

The most common error beginners make is focusing on seducing a
woman *before* attracting her. This is putting the cart before the horse.
Often, to beautiful women in particular, seduction first is little more
than the equivalent of saying, "You don't know me, but will you sleep
with me?" There is a time (and a place) to begin the seduction stage,
but it's not until you first have attraction and comfort, not to mention
privacy.

Seducers mistakenly begin at the end. Like the typical guy, they often blatantly disregard a woman's comfort levels entirely. Even if there
is a level of attraction based on the seducer's appearance alone, this is
superseded by her discomfort in having to deal with aggressive sexual
advances from someone she doesn't know or trust. It is best to not
prematurely telegraph strong sexual interest until end-game.

Fool's Mate

In the game of chess, it is possible to win in only four moves. This gambit is called **fool's mate.** Winning with speed via fool's mate does not, however, make you a chess champion. If anything, it only demonstrates your opponent's inexperience. An experienced chess player will not even attempt a fast fool's mate because if his opponent doesn't take the bait, he himself is left vulnerable. Similarly, while it is possible to seduce with speed, it is much less probable on a woman who is socially experienced. In the Venusian arts, we refer metaphorically to seduction-first tactics as fool's mate. In contrast, both chess champions and Venusian artists prefer to play a **solid game.**

Fool's mate can work in some situations that may be acceptable to you, such as on girls who have a propensity toward having one-night stands. Just don't let it be your only winning move.

SEQUENCING MISTAKE #2: TO START IN THE MIDDLE

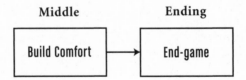

The Nice Guy

Many men understand and appreciate that seduction first makes women feel uncomfortable. What these men do instead is focus on comfort first.

What these men don't realize is that women of beauty get bombarded by these **nice guys** every day and it can grow quite tiresome. While not as offensive as the seducer, the nice guy is no less a bother. There are simply too many nice guys approaching them in a day to indulge in the same old lengthy dialogue time after time. Without attraction first, simply saying, "Hi, I'm Joe. What's your name?" will smack of every nice guy before you. Why would a woman who isn't attracted to you care what your name is or bother to even remember it? Why would she divulge personal information just because you asked?

The Protection Shield Metaphor

If a woman is not attracted to you, any attempt at comfort building will bore her. Telling her about you, getting her to talk about herself, and complimenting her before she deserves it are all comfort-building attempts. If you've ever been trapped in a conversation with someone with whom you weren't interested, you'll understand how uncomfortable it can be.

Imagine this happening to you several times a day, almost every day, for many years. Wouldn't you recognize the need to shut these people down before they even got started? Over time, as a woman interacts with ever more nice guys, she begins to evolve simple-yet-effective strategies for countering this barrage of bore. Collectively, these strategies make up what is metaphorically called her **protection shield** (more on that in chapter 5).

Telegraphing Sexual Interest

Simply by approaching them and being nice, you suggest to women of beauty that you want something from them. If the woman doesn't think you are selling something (or begging for change), she'll reason it's because you want to win her sexual favor. Even if you *aren't* interested in her sexually, she'll assume you are, just because you approached her in the same manner as the last half-dozen nice guys did that night.

Him: *Nice boots.*
Her: *I have a boyfriend.*

Most men mistake these short-term defenses for long-term personality flaws. This strategy quite often successfully turns men off—and it is for this very reason that it works for a woman. From her perspective it's better to allow a bunch of men she's not attracted to to think she's a bitch than to have to sit there and listen to them all.

> **Him:** *What's your name?*
> **Her:** *Get lost.*

Some woman may tolerate mildly entertaining nice-guy dialogue, but once the conversation begins to grow mundane, they'll excuse themselves. Persistent nice guys will meet greater resistance as they become weary of these men's prolonged presence. Although playing a bitch can become a form of entertainment for some, most women with protection shields use them for good reason and are otherwise very nice people.

> **Him:** *Hi, how are you?*
> **Her:** *Look, I'm not going to have sex with you.*

If you don't take the time to attract a woman first, you won't give her a reason to want to even have a conversation with you. It will force her to raise her shields. Keep comfort building in mid-game. Don't begin prematurely in the middle.

SEQUENCING MISTAKE #3: TO START AT THE BEGINNING BUT SKIP THE MIDDLE AND GO STRAIGHT TO THE END

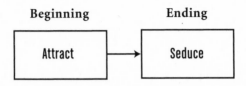

Every beginning and ending has a middle, and in M3 that middle is comfort. There is a time to seduce a girl (or be seduced), but it's not until after you have built comfort.

THE PLAYER

A player is a Venusian artist who begins at the beginning and successfully attracts a girl but fails to avoid the three **player traps.** Every Venusian artist must be aware of them:

1. Failure to justify a mutual attraction
2. Disregard of comfort
3. Buyer's remorse

Player Trap#1: Failure to Justify a Mutual Attraction

Justifiably to men, a woman's beauty can be so intoxicating that it alone qualifies her as girlfriend material. But we cannot let her know we're choosing her based on looks because it doesn't seem genuine and makes us appear like other typical men.

A woman's **indicators of interest (IOIs)** notify when to go from the attraction stage to the comfort stage, but you must not do so until she has legitimately earned *your* IOIs as well! Getting IOIs from a woman is simply not enough reason to begin returning them. If you are too easy, she will mark you as another notch in her belt and move on in search of more challenging conquests.

Some examples of IOIs:

- She asks you for your name.
- She touches you. When you say, "Hands off the merchandise," she touches you again.
- When you grab her hands and hold them, she holds back.
- She laughs at all your humorous remarks—and the ones that aren't funny as well.
- When you ask her to bite your neck, she does.

You must first encourage her to demonstrate qualities that can substantiate your attraction. If you don't, she may suspect that you only played with her emotions, callously attracting her in a game to win another score. She will feel uncomfortable being attracted to you, and as a result she will lose this attraction for you quickly. Your attraction-stage dialogue will in fact be viewed as conniving, and she will perceive you as being emotionally manipulative. In this light, a player is simply a seducer with good opening game.

Having successfully negotiated beyond the first *player trap*, the Venusian artist can then move on to comfort building.

Player Trap #2: Disregard of Comfort

If you attempt to seduce a woman before building sufficient comfort, her attraction switches for you will turn off. To keep this from happening, you must build enough comfort so your seduction won't make her feel uncomfortable. Do not cross the line from comfort to seduction until you have developed enough comfort.

THE SEVEN-HOUR RULE When do you know you have enough comfort to begin seduction? It takes an average of four to ten hours of cumulative comfort building before a woman is ready for seduction. (Not counting fool's mate—which, as I said earlier, is a strategy to be avoided by true Venusian artists.) There is no black-and-white rule for determining when that moment has arrived. Only your calibration can tell you that. (More on the Seven-Hour Rule later.)

The Seven Hour Rule

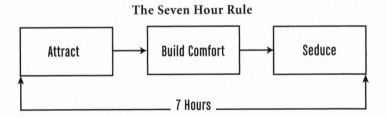

Player Trap #3: Buyer's Remorse

Buyer's remorse occurs when a person purchases something on a whim, only to regret the purchase later. Similarly, a woman who is attracted to you may be pushed or, on her own, go too far too soon.

While in the moment she may indulge in her attraction and sexual arousal, only to regret her feelings or actions later. Assuming you want to reach the seduction phase, buyer's remorse is something you want to avoid at all costs.

A Case Study: Jim Meets Janine

THE MAN'S POINT OF VIEW

Jim meets a beautiful woman named Janine, and they build attraction for each other. Jim soon finds himself making out with her that night. It's getting hot and heavy, but unable to go somewhere private at that time, they exchange numbers, and agree to see each other another night. He excitedly tells his buddies that he just met his next girlfriend.

Jim calls Janine the next evening, but she is cold and unresponsive on the phone. He tries to convince her to see him as they agreed, but she's now "busy." He leaves several messages, but Janine never returns a single call. Weeks pass, and Jim and Janine never get together again. He is left confused, frustrated, and alone. Worse, he repeats this painful pattern over and over with other women.

This scenario is typical of how an otherwise great guy succumbs to the buyer's remorse trap. Many have fallen into it repeatedly and lost countless opportunities at love. I provide a free forum at *www.mysterymethod.com/forum/* where aspiring Venusian artists may post field reports and learn from one another. This is a tale that—until they get good—men repeat all the time.

WHAT WENT WRONG?

Here's what happened.

THE WOMAN'S POINT OF VIEW

While Janine did enjoy making out with Jim, he did not take it upon himself to slow down the sexual escalation and remain in the comfort-building stage. She truly did wish to see him again, but only in the moment. When Jim called the next day, Janine wasn't in the same aroused emotional state as the night before. Due to cultural programming, she felt a little guilty for doing what she did with someone she didn't really know. She knew the only reason Jim even called was to continue something that she was now uncomfortable just thinking about. If she did see him again, she didn't know how he would behave. Would he grope her and make her feel even more uncomfortable? She just didn't know him well enough to trust his future actions. Being one to indulge in her emotions, she allowed them to once again make her decisions. Uncomfortable even talking to him on the phone, Janine was cold to him and lied, saying she was too busy to talk.

When the confused Jim tried to change her mind, Janine took this as an attempt to manipulate her. She just didn't want to be pressured into having sex with someone with whom she didn't feel comfortable and safe, especially when she was not even aroused.

Jim was hard-pressed to change her emotional state on the phone. For all he knew at the time, with so many elements out of his control, Janine may have just had a fight with her roommate or just changed the kitty litter box. Over the next week or two, every time he left a message, her feelings of discomfort grew. She had no intention of ever seeing this guy again.

Jim shouldn't blame Janine for "stringing him along." After all, it was he who ultimately created this situation by not remaining in the comfort stage for an appropriate length of time.

As hand-holding escalates to kissing (more on how to perform *Mystery's kiss gambit* later), you will quickly approach a point of no return regarding buyer's remorse.

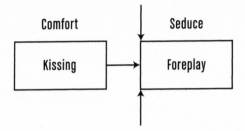

BEWARE: The Buyer's Remorse Point of No Return

This point of no return exists where kissing turns into foreplay without enough comfort.

> **✦ KISS:**
> *To touch or caress with the lips as a mark of affection (or greeting)*
> *Etymology: Middle English, from Old English cyssan; akin to*
> *Old High German kussen to kiss*
> *Date: before 12th century*

> **✦ FOREPLAY:**
> *Mutual sexual stimulation preceding intercourse*
> *Date: 1929*
>
> *—Merriam-Webster's Dictionary*, 10th ed.

Note how a choice you make at one time will determine the outcome of a situation a day or more later. *Beware!* Once you cross the point of no return, unless you have enough comfort established to get her to a nearby private location to have sex with her (before her arousal wanes), she will later get buyer's remorse.

Only a seducer considers the option of taking her to a nearby bathroom stall. Further consider that if your girlfriend of two years wouldn't feel comfortable having sex with you in a public bathroom, don't expect someone you met just twenty minutes ago to do it, no matter how aroused she is. This is a **fool's mate fantasy** and not solid

game. You may lose an otherwise great opportunity if you push for seduction too soon. (Although on the rare occasion that the two of you
are willing, enjoy yourself.)

Nonsexual intimate kissing is a welcomed comfort-stage action. **In
fact, if you wait too long to kiss her, she will at some point become uninterested and you will lose the opportunity to kiss her in the future.**

Generally, this type of "comfort kissing" lasts less than thirty seconds and does not include tongue. Kissing, on the one hand, expresses
and builds a sense of connection. Foreplay, on the other hand, belongs
in the seduction stage only. Generally, this consists of French-kissing,
which leads to sexual touching. It sexually arouses both parties in
preparation for sex.

It's best not to begin foreplay until you have the comfort and privacy necessary to transition naturally to sex. As kissing prematurely
turns to foreplay, it's time to push her off of you. When doing so, let
her know that it's neither the right time nor the right place to be getting too hot and heavy. Agreeably, such self-restraint is very tough, and
it is at this point that many men fail.

To help avoid this pitfall, ask yourself this one very serious question:
"Do I want one night of petting, or countless nights of sex?"

To know whether you are nearing the point of no return, ask yourself: "Is this foreplay?" If the answer is yes, stop! Push her away. Build
comfort, not arousal. It takes a real man with reserve to say, "Whoa, we
better stop. Come on; let's rejoin our friends." "*Our* friends" may really
be "*her* friends." With this winning move you build trust by demonstrating you want to get to know her for more than mere sexual favors.
Since her sexual attraction to you is now apparent, you may feel secure
in that fact when you have established enough comfort to get her into
a private seduction location, such as your bedroom. You may then sexually arouse her and allow nature to take its course *unimpeded.*

You may build intimacy and get close to the point of no return several times, so long as you are the first to push her away each time
you've approached it.

SEQUENCING MISTAKE #4: TO START AT THE BEGINNING BUT GET STUCK IN THE MIDDLE

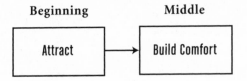

The Friendship Zone

The **friend** has a very specific connotation in the Game. It is someone who fears expressing his romantic intent to a woman he has spent time getting to know.

If you fail to convey to a woman that you are a potential romantic interest to her during the comfort stage, she may not be intuitive enough to see that in fact you are one. Not holding her hands, smelling her neck, or kissing her during the comfort stage can trap you there. In fact, a woman may grow so comfortable with your nonsexual nature that she will prefer you stay that way. When you finally attempt to move into the seduction stage with a woman and you hear her say, "Let's just be friends," you are trapped in the **friendship zone.**

You cannot begin seduction until you end the comfort stage, but you cannot do *that* until you have built sufficient comfort and familiarity. And she must be comfortable with your sexuality, too. This occurs when kissing her does not make her feel uncomfortable. When you are alone with her and you begin the seduction stage, you don't want her to be shocked by your *sudden sexual interest.*

As you avoid the friendship zone like a disease, know that it is neither wrongful nor a sin to structure an opportunity for mutual seduction. After all, building a sexual relationship together will benefit her, too.

Is There an Escape Route?

What if you find yourself stuck in the friendship zone with a highly prized target? Is there still hope, or is all lost? Let me put it this way: If a woman does not give you IOIs by the twenty-fifth minute of your interaction, your first impression is blown to smithereens. If you're twenty hours in and she's a friend who feels uncomfortable with any physical escalation, don't expect to demonstrate higher value all of a sudden and get the girl. She already knows that you don't have the value that she wants. And since she already has her friendship with you, she doesn't have to give up the value she's already getting.

At that point, if you still desire this target, the only thing you can do is take yourself away from her for a while—and then come back a new man. You're going to have to demonstrate higher value, and the only way you can do that is by showing an improvement in your S-and-R value. Move to a new apartment, get a hot new car—basically, reinvent yourself. You have to show her that you're no longer the same person. Most important, you need to come back with a new girl as well to build in a jealousy plotline. She could have had you but chose not to, and now that she can't have you again, she will want you.

Make no mistake: Demonstrating higher value under these circumstances is really hard. In fact, it's harder than going back to square one, because now you have to prove to her that you have value that she already *knows* you don't have. Forget about merely *projecting* higher value; now you must actually possess it. If you're not willing to go to such great lengths, just keep her as a friend, but forget seducing her. She doesn't see value in you—hence, it won't happen. Move on to a fresh target.

SUMMARY: PROBLEMS ASSOCIATED WITH IMPROPER M3 SEQUENCING

1. Starting at the end = *fool's mate* problems
2. Starting at the middle = *protection shield* problems
3. Starting at the beginning but skipping the middle = *buyer's remorse* problems
4. Starting at the beginning but getting stuck in the middle = *friendship zone* problems

GAMING LOCATIONS

A solid-game courtship that ends in sex will rarely, *if ever,* take place in its entirety in only one physical location. It is highly improbable that a woman you have never met before will knock on your bedroom door and invite herself in. Nature demands that you leave your bedroom and travel to a different location where meeting her is much more probable. This is where many lonely men fail miserably.

There are in fact three separate location types you and your romantic interest will likely visit (or *jump* to):

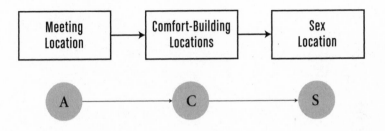

LOCATION CHANGES

There are three types of location changes, or *jumps,* that commonly occur while gaming. They are the **move,** the **bounce,** and the **time bridge.** Briefly described here, these location changes are covered in greater detail in the subsequent chapters of this book.

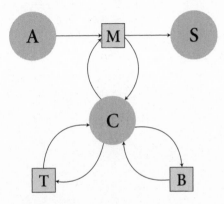

M	-MOVE	**MOVE**

MOVE

Move the girl to a different area of the current venue.

B	-BOUNCE

BOUNCE

You and the girl exit the current venue together, and go to a different venue together.

T	-TIME BRIDGE

TIME BRIDGE

Sometimes it is not possible to escalate. Perhaps some outside factor requires you to exchange contact information and continue gaming the girl at a later time and place. This is called a time bridge.

THE NINE PHASES OF THE M3 MODEL

The three stages of the M3 Model—Attract, Build Comfort, and Seduce—are in turn broken down into three phases each. Though they are briefly described here, the nine phases of the M3 Model are covered in much greater detail in the subsequent chapters of this book.

A1-OPEN	C1-CONVERSATION	S1-FOREPLAY
A2-FEMALE-TO-MALE INTEREST	C2-CONNECTION	S2-LMR
A3-MALE-TO-FEMALE INTEREST	C3-INTIMACY	S3-SEX

A1-OPEN

The man approaches a set, runs an opener, and immediately earns the set's acceptance.

A2-FEMALE-TO-MALE INTEREST

The man demonstrates higher value, while simultaneously showing lack of interest in the target. She responds with indicators of interest.

A3-MALE-TO-FEMALE INTEREST

The man baits the woman to become more invested in the interaction, and then he rewards her efforts with indicators of interest.

C1-CONVERSATION

The couple shares in friendly dialogue. A sense of comfort and rapport develops.

C2-CONNECTION

Both parties feel a vibe that "it is on." Kissing occurs. This phase may last over the course of several dates.

C3-INTIMACY

Now at a seduction location, heavy making out ensues and the couple moves into the bedroom.

S1-FOREPLAY

The couple begins the physical escalation toward sex. If this happens too soon, it can cause buyer's remorse.

S2-LMR

Last-minute resistance is the point of no return before sex occurs. It's often a freak-out moment for the woman.

C3-SEX

It is necessary to have sexual intercourse several times in order to ensure a sexual relationship.

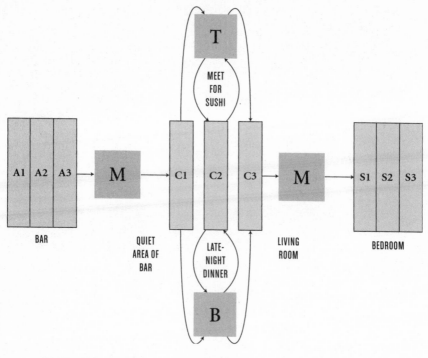

PUTTING IT ALL TOGETHER

A1. A Venusian artist with tight game approaches a set of people in a bar, using an indirect opener. He doesn't seem needy or interested in the target and in fact comes across as though he's just leaving. He then demonstrates higher value to the set and crosses the social hook point, the point at which they accept him.

A2. He continues to convey his personality using stories, humor, patterns, games, routines, palm reading, poetry, etc. This, combined with his apparent lack of interest in the target, raises his social value relative to hers and intensifies her emotional state. She begins to give him indicators of interest.

A3, C1. He uses takeaways to bait her into chasing after him to earn his affections. As she becomes more invested in the interaction, he rewards her with indicators of interest. Then he moves her to a quiet area of the bar to begin building comfort.

C2, C3. With a bounce to Mel's Diner and a time bridge for sushi the next day, he builds comfort, connection, and trust over a cumulative seven-hour period. At some point during C2 they begin kissing. They eventually bounce to his apartment.

S1, S2, S3. Finally, he moves her into his bedroom, begins foreplay, overcomes any last-minute resistance, and has sex with her.

REVIEW

+ The Game is played in the field. Get out there.
+ **The MM Newbie Drill**
    Go out gaming four nights per week for four hours each
        night.
    Make three approaches per hour.
    Post your results (and read about others') on the Venusian
        Arts Forum (www.themysterymethod.com/forum).
+ Gaming is like golfing or fishing. You must enjoy the process
    and release expectation from outcome in order to get the best
    results in the long term.
+ Every sexual relationship has a beginning, middle, and ending.
    The beginning is known as **courtship.**
+ Courtship has three stages, known as the **pickup, mid-game,**
    and **end-game.**
+ Mystery Method focuses on attraction first, not seduction.
    Ethically, practitioners of the Mystery Method are attractors,
    not seducers.
+ There are certain hardwired attraction switches in every
    woman's mind. Attraction is not a conscious choice that people
    make. Rather, it's a response that they feel automatically as a re-
    sult of these switches being flipped.
+ The **preselection** switch gets triggered when a woman sees that
    you have already been preapproved by other women.
+ The M3 Model describes the structure of the courtship as oc-
    curring in three steps: **Attract, Build Comfort,** and **Seduce.** It is
    necessary to build comfort before you can seduce a woman,
    and it is necessary to build attraction before she will bother to
    build comfort with you.
+ While you are comfort building, it is important to convey to
    the woman that you are a sexual man and a potential romantic
    interest. Otherwise you can get trapped in the **friendship zone.**

- The phenomenon where you occasionally get sex even when you haven't built enough comfort is known as **fool's mate.**
- Women have certain strategies, built up over time, that enable them to avoid constant approaches from men. This is known as the **protection shield.** Even though a woman is probably a nice person, she can sometimes appear bitchy as a result. It's not who she really is.
- The three stages of the M3 Model are broken down into three phases each: A1: Open; A2: Female-to-Male Interest; A3: Male-to-Female Interest; C1: Conversation; C2: Connection; C3: Intimacy; S1: Foreplay; S2: LMR (Last-Minute Resistance); S3: Sex.
- There are three types of locations: the meeting location, the comfort-building locations, and the sex location.
- There are three types of location changes or *jumps*: **the move, the bounce,** and **the time bridge.**
- The **pickup** occurs at the **meeting location** and covers the phases A1, A2, A3, and C1. It usually includes at least one move and ends with a bounce or time bridge.
- The next stage, called **mid-game,** occurs in one or several **comfort-building locations** and covers the C2 phase. Various bounces and time bridges may occur here. When this stage is over, you will be with her in the seduction location and you've already been somewhat intimate with her (kissing, etc.).
- The final stage, called **end-game,** begins in C3 but soon shifts into S1 **(foreplay.)** Often **last-minute resistance** (S2) will come up, which is normal, followed by sex (S3). If you initiate foreplay before enough comfort has been built, it will cause **buyer's remorse.**
- It is necessary to have sex several times before the sexual relationship is ensured. During and even after this point she will continue testing you for congruence.

5.

A1: OPEN

*Opening a set and crossing the social
hook point without conveying neediness*

Once you begin talking to a set of girls, the immediate goal is to reach the social acceptance, or hook, point. A moment comes when the set decides that they enjoy talking to you and that they want to continue talking to you. When this happens, you have successfully opened the set and finished A1. It's easy to tell when this happens because there will be **indicators of interest.**

THE MEETING LOCATION

Any location in which there is a high probability of meeting women is called a **meeting location.** While it is *possible* to meet a beautiful woman virtually anywhere, even on the street, it is more *probable* to meet her in a public gathering.

Meeting locations are gatherings in which people self-organize into small groups of usually two to five friends each.

Examples:

+ Restaurants and busy cafés
+ Pubs, bars, and nightclubs

✦ Busy stores, malls, and outdoor festivals

✦ Parties and get-togethers

The Unconscious Replication Agenda

People often publicly assemble to drink, mingle, dance, shop, or eat. While some know they are out specifically to seek a mate, many are unaware that their unconscious mind has imposed a hidden replication agenda upon them. Even though women know these gatherings are chock-full of pestering nice guys, most are unconscious of the fact that, nonetheless, their emotional circuitry has a replication agenda compelling them to actively socialize, such as when women go out "just to dance." This is a perfect example of **rationalization** at work.

Attractive Women Are Found in Groups

Seldom will you see women of beauty alone in such locations. Many have grown accustomed to the constant threat of nice guys who plague these gatherings. Women learn to band together with trusted friends to help protect them from these everyday public nuisances.

A meeting location is said to be **target rich** if it offers multiple approach opportunities with attractive women in short succession, whereas a location with few such opportunities is said to be **target poor**. Target-rich environments not only improve your chances of finding and attracting a beautiful woman; they also substantially accelerate your learning curve by providing more chances to practice your social skills in less time. There's nothing about the Mystery

> **Specialty Game: Hired Guns**
>
> You may thank the management of many meeting locations for hiring attractive women because they have performed the difficult task of finding these women for you. These beautiful hired guns include seating hostesses, shooter girls, bartenders, promotional models, sports-bar waitresses, go-go and other exotic dancers. I have personally dated many hired guns and enjoy sharing my special techniques for picking them up in my weekend seminar titled Mystery on Hired Guns. (A current schedule can be found at www.mysterymethod.com. Hired-gun game is challenging and very rewarding. It's not harder to pick up a hired gun, only different.

Method that requires clubs or target-rich environments (it works just as well in the grocery store or the coffee shop), but they definitely make it easier to practice. For this reason, our boot camps (where we take a small number of guys out to teach them the Venusian arts and interact with beautiful women in the field) generally take place in lounges, clubs, and restaurants.

Proactively go to four or five of the very best meeting locations in your city ahead of time. Go on an off night. Scope them out. Acclimate and desensitize yourself to the environment in which you will train and game. Public gatherings are the Venusian artist's dojo.

PROXIMITY

When you are in the field, a shy woman, reluctant even to make eye contact with you, may find you appealing and, at either a conscious or unconscious level, reveal her interest via **proximity,** or nearness.

Typically, if a girl is giving off an IOI through proximity, she will stand five to eight feet away from you, facing away. Dynamic social homeostasis brings her within range to observe you and welcome your possible approach—but prevents her from coming too close.

With proximity, if you open her, she will open receptively.

Have you ever walked into a nightclub and found yourself standing near a woman you were attracted to, if only to be near her and check her out more? Maybe instead of approaching her, you ordered a drink at the bar right next to her. Have you ever been in a store shopping where it seemed that a woman you had seen earlier stood near you several times over a short period of time? Her repeated proximity indicates a potential interest. She may be putting herself near you on purpose, hoping you might start something. **It's also quite possible that her replication circuitry is placing her near you, even though she is not consciously aware of what her body is doing.** She will still open receptively. These opportunities occur with more frequency than you may expect, especially if you are already working a set of girls.

THE THREE-SECOND RULE

Approaching a group of strangers can be uncomfortable in the short term, but the feeling that persists after you see a beautiful woman you could have approached but didn't lasts as long and is equally as uncomfortable. Know your opener ahead of time, even before you have entered the public gathering. **Within three seconds of spotting a woman you are attracted to, you must open her set.** The approach must be reactionary, and this is what the Venusian artist trains for. Decide now to train for this, and internalize the Three-Second Rule. Just walk right up to the set of people that you see and open them before your approach anxiety exceeds your desire to make her your girlfriend. At our live programs, we show you how to do this (in real situations, so you're doing it live) and blow away approach anxiety. For now, you're just going to have to force yourself through this.

Keep in mind that no one else in the venue knows whom you already know and don't know. It certainly *seems* as if you know them—after all, you entered the venue and walked right up to them, and now they are enjoying a fun conversation with you. From the perspective of adjacent sets, it appears you must be a social guy with lots of friends!

As you eventually move from one set to the next, this positive perception of you continues to grow. You are becoming **socially proofed** in the venue. Notice the ease with which sets open up to you when you have this level of social proof. For this reason, it is important not to be too selective in choosing your sets early in the night; better to be in any set than to get picky and end up alone when you could have been working the room. You don't always have to have a legitimate target to enjoy interacting with people.

This really adds a natural spontaneity to your approach. A woman can usually tell it a mile away when a man is working up the courage to approach her, which can lower his perceived value. If you follow the Three-Second Rule, she will feel like you just popped up out of nowhere. A very nice energy is added to the interaction when following this rule.

THE THREE-MINUTE EXCEPTION

What if you see a group, and the target you single out is talking to the waitress? Should you still open within three seconds? No. There are commonsense exceptions to every rule, and this is one of them. If a group of people comes into a restaurant and sits down, I'm not going to go in if I feel there will be an external interrupt coming within the first three minutes of opening the set. If I don't have three minutes to work, I can't lock myself into the set. Once I am locked in I can handle external interruptions like a waitress approaching, because I'll be locked in by then. However, if she comes when I'm a minute and a half into the set, it can completely disrupt things.

The disruption can also be internal, or coming from within the set. For example, if a target is standing in a line and I can tell she is not going to stay there for more than a minute, I'm not going to go in at that point. Instead, I'll hold back and wait for her to sit down. Then I can go in with confidence that I won't have an interruption during the first three minutes of my approach.

OPENERS

An **opener** is a short story or statement used to get a group's attention and earn their acceptance of your presence. It is not a time to formally introduce yourself or hit on the hot girl in the set.

Using a **direct opener** such as, "Wow, you are beautiful; my name is Glen," may convey confidence, but it also alienates your target's friends if present. Since women of beauty are rarely found alone, we must engage the entire group without hitting on the girl prematurely.

For this reason Venusian artists make effective use of an **indirect opener.** Here is an indirect opener of mine that opened nearly every mixed set I ran it on:

Mystery: *Oh my God. Did you guys see the girl fight outside?*
Girls: *[Cut them off before they speak.]*

Mystery: *They were fighting over this guy. I talked to him afterward. His name was Glen. That's a deal-breaker name. Glen. So they were pulling each other's hair and one of the girls' boobs pops out. Normally I'm all for seeing a ripe one, but this was a "saggy-baggy booby"* . . . *you know, from* National Geographic.

Go immediately into next routine.

You may feel this dialogue won't miraculously make a woman fall for you, and you are right. It's not designed to. Sure, it's designed to be fun and appear spontaneous, but the power of this gambit comes from what it doesn't do. Unlike a typical direct opener, no IOIs are conveyed to the target. To do so at this time would surely compromise your chances of survival were you to hit on the married woman with her husband present. We must discover the group's relationship dynamics *before* giving IOIs. This approach will make you appear naturally confident and not insecurely bold. Notice there is no talk about the fact that you are presently speaking to them. It is designed to convey personality first.

IN THE VENUE

Bars and clubs are probably not the venues where you plan to find your future wife. Nevertheless, these are **target-rich** environments and thus are perfect for practicing the Game. Here are some tips:

+ **Don't buy her a drink**: As a general rule—but not a dogmatic one—don't offer to buy drinks for girls. If she asks you to buy her a drink, turn her down. Although you can break this rule, it's preferable to get your game so tight that *she* will be buying *you* drinks.
+ **Be willing to crash and burn** every set for the entire night. Do it for fun with your wing.
+ **Give your wing two hundred dollars.** Then he gives you twenty dollars every time you approach a set. This game is very effective.

- Be willing to **go out alone** if you have to.
- **Don't hold your drink in front of your chest** like a security blanket. Hold it low to your hip. Better yet, don't hold one at all.
- **Don't try to look "cool" or "tough."** You will just look bored and boring. Instead, be comfortable and friendly.
- **Enthusiasm** is contagious.
- **Smile** as you walk around the venue. Guys who don't have success with women don't smile.
- **Once you open a set, stop smiling so much.** You don't want to appear **try-hard.**
- You ran your opener, but the set didn't hook? Run another one. **Stack your material** if for no other reason than to get practice. Stacking routines is a useful skill in and of itself.
- It usually takes **three warm-up approaches** to really get in a talkative personality-conveying groove.
- **Avoid noisy areas.** If you can't talk, you can't run game. Find the quietest areas of the club. And avoid the dance floor—it's a trap.
- **Arrive early** and be friendly with the staff. At midnight, bounce to another club. This keeps the crowd fresh and gives you somewhere to take girls whom you've been gaming.
- **Don't drink** or at least cut back. If you go out gaming without alcohol, you will really notice an improvement in your abilities. Alcohol is not a legitimate tool for handling your anticipatory anxiety.
- **Guys are just ugly girls:** Yes, there are other guys at the venue, but they aren't competition. They don't smile; they don't surround themselves with people who are talking and laughing. Instead, they hold a beer to their chest and try to "look cool." These guys are not really competition.
- **Befriend the social guys** and practice gaming them. One of the attraction switches in women is the **leader-of-men** switch. **When you lead the men, the women will follow.**
- **Be the observed:** There are constantly little *events* going on in the field: A flash goes off as a group of people pose for a picture.

A man teaches a woman a little dance move. A group of people busts up laughing. A girl gasps at an impressive and flashy routine, and people nearby look over to see what is going on. Are you the *observer* when these things happen or the *observed*?

THE PROTECTION SHIELD

Women use many strategies to protect themselves from men with a low perceived S-and-R value:

* a ring
* saying they have a boyfriend
* surrounding themselves with friends
* sitting in a place where it is hard to approach them
* being bitchy, using insults
* negative body language
* no eye contact
* lack of interest
* being bubbly and wanting to dance
* no sense of humor
* being defensive

Collectively, these strategies amount to a unique *shield* that each woman uses to protect herself. The components of the shields that women deploy can range from subtle and mild-mannered to in-your-face and cruel. Many years ago I had a girl literally scream at me to fuck off as I tried to open her set. If it ever happens to you, move on, and don't take it personally. Sometimes women are just having a very bad day.

The opening phase is the time that it takes you to get past the shield and reach the acceptance point. You might try pushing through the shield with persistence, even though the woman is treating you poorly (albeit not screaming at you to fuck off, I hope), but this short-sighted tactic diminishes your value.

Instead, what if you can trick her into lowering her shield? This means making the woman believe you are not here to steal her eggs. She must think that you aren't even considering seducing her.

You may enter her set with a **pawn**. A pawn is a girl whom you have gamed previously for the express purpose of bringing her into your next set, so that it will open more easily. The use of pawns has been known to lower protection shields.

Other ways to get through the shield include usage of **uninterested body language** and **false time constraints**. These techniques are described in detail in this chapter.

Notice that all of these tactics have one thing in common: *They convey lack of interest.* In other words, women aren't so shielded against men who have a *willingness to walk.* Women feel safe around those men.

Whatever happens, it's crucial that you *not be affected* by a woman's shielding behavior, no matter how unacceptable such behavior may be. If she is able to shake your internal sense of reality, your value will drop in her eyes. Never get angry—just stay in a good mood and be unaffected. *It's no big deal.*

As you demonstrate value and an utter lack of neediness, she will start to open up to you. How will you know that you have disarmed her shield?

- When she laughs at your jokes—even the bad ones
- When she turns to face you, makes eye contact, and is responsive to you
- When she touches you—usually a soft grab of your arm, leg, necklace, or hair
- When she asks you your name

CANNED MATERIAL

The Mystery Method incorporates the use of **canned material.** If a particular *value-demonstrating routine* has been internalized and is ready for use in set, then that routine is said to be **in the can.**

A Venusian artist who can deliver canned material properly will be able to generate consistent, powerful responses while he is "in set." It is a potent tool. Of course, no single tool should ever become a crutch—it's also vitally important for the open-minded Venusian artist to practice spontaneous, natural conversation. After all, that's where the best-canned material comes from in the first place. Nevertheless, your skill set is incomplete without the ability to deliver canned material congruently.

I recommend that you create a **routine stack** of canned material that you can practice in the field when you are starting out; that is, an opener, a few routines, and so on. Although certain stock routines and even powerful, field-tested gambits are traded online and are available in books, in the longer term you must develop your own material.

While you are practicing and internalizing your routine stack, approaches start to become a blur. Patterns emerge over time. Situations and reactions become easily predictable before they occur. Social challenges are discovered and solved. It will seem like you're moving at hyperspeed while the world around you slows to a crawl. Ever seen the movie version of *Spider-Man*? The spider has already bitten Peter Parker when a bully throws a punch at him, and when Peter leans back to get out of the way, from his perspective, it's all happening in slow motion. He thinks, *Wow, I've got all this time to react.*

That's how I feel "in set," and that's how you can feel, too. It's amazing to go into a set and *literally* get every girl you choose to approach. That's true mastery. And yes, true Venusian arts mastery is a superpower.

Once you have performed a particular story or routine dozens of times, you don't even have to think about what you are saying. Your mind is free for other tasks, such as planning the next move. You have already fully explored all the conversational threads that could possibly arise from this piece of material. It's almost like seeing the future.

PROPER DELIVERY OF MATERIAL

The delivery of canned material is often more important than the content. Women have a finely tuned intuition for the subtle behaviors of a man with high S-and-R value: his eye contact, tone of voice, body language, and so on.

The use of canned material allows you to automate the verbal aspects of the interaction to some extent, so that you have more of an opportunity to practice the delivery. Once this improved delivery has been internalized, even your natural, spontaneous conversations will benefit. **Your delivery itself will become a demonstration of higher value.**

Expressiveness

Many beginners are not as expressive as they need to be to convey a confident personality. They should focus on animated facial expressions and vocal tonality. If they were to increase their level of expressiveness to where it actually needs to be, it would *feel* as if it's too much. This feeling can be deceptive.

Gaming with a higher energy level makes it easier to hook sets. In fact, beginners can become addicted to the powerful responses they can generate by running game with emotionally expressive vocal tonality and facial expressions. Of course, a well-rounded Venusian artist should be capable of hooking sets at lower energy levels as well.

When you are first opening a set, it's important to come in at an energy level slightly higher than that of the set. If you come in at lower energy than is already in the set, you are only going into their set to bring them down. They won't be interested.

If your energy is too low, sets will not hook. If your energy is too high, sets will easily hook, but closing will be more difficult and girls will more often accuse you of being gay. But when you open with the right energy level, sets will hook and lead to solid closes much more consistently. Only time in the field will give you the calibration to know exactly how much energy is appropriate for a particular set.

False Time Constraints

When you open a set, you haven't yet had much time to build value, and thus you are nearly indistinguishable from every other loser guy.

A girl might think, *Oh great, how long is this guy going to be here? Am I going to have to go dance, or go to the bathroom, or go buy a drink so that I can get rid of this guy?*

This frame of mind is not a useful one for her to be in. But it is possible to inoculate her mind against such thoughts. You can create the illusion in her mind that you are just leaving anyway. She should always feel like you are about to leave in A1.

One way of creating this impression is through **false time constraints** or FTCs. Here are a few examples:

- "You know what . . . if I didn't have to go right now—which I do—I would . . ."
- "I can only stay a sec, I'm here with friends, so check this out. . . ."
- "I've only got a minute, so I've got to tell you about . . ."

After you deliver the first few words of your opener, use a false time constraint. Then once you reach the hook point, try delivering another false time constraint. Why? Because the set has now decided that they want you to stay. A false time constraint at this moment will create a fear of loss. Thus begins the cycle of baiting the target to chase.

Body Rocking

Body rocking is the use of physical movement to create the impression that you are just about to leave the set. In other words, it's a nonverbal false time constraint. You must make those in the set feel like you are not staying long. As you speak, begin to turn away and shift your weight to your back leg like you are about to leave, then return as you say, "Oh, by the way, before I go . . . ," and stack to your next story or routine.

It's not good to have a lot of extra motion while you are in set, and some beginners have a problem with bouncing around or fidgeting. Beware: Usually this sort of motion is unconscious, and it expresses nervous energy. Without a faithful wing to point this out, you may not even realize you are doing it. Movement like this can wreck an otherwise perfectly good set.

The person who moves the least (i.e., the person who reacts the least) will often be perceived as the one with more social status. If you are not moving for a calculated reason, such as for performing body rocking, then it is better to stay in one spot, with a comfortable body posture. Avoid fidgeting.

Opening Moving Sets

Some girls are walking through the venue. Is your game strong enough to stop them with your opener?

It is extremely difficult to open moving sets consistently. The most important principle to remember is that the girls should never perceive you as chasing them. If they do, then you will come across as having lower value and they will leave. One way to avoid this is to remain firmly rooted to the ground when opening. Don't step into her.

Alternately, consider that **an object in motion tends to remain in motion.** Here is the MM technique for opening moving sets:

1. Walk along the same trajectory as the set, *slightly in front of them.*
2. Turn your head back toward the set, run an opener, and then look forward as you speak.
3. Continue walking beside the set and gaming them. Slow down and watch them match your pacing.

Opening Seated Sets

Upon first opening a seated set, everything seems fine. You stand near the set, running material that is apparently well received. But as time passes, you begin to lose their attention. Where did you go wrong?

In standing, while the rest of the set are seated, you have less physical comfort than they do. This betrays a subtext that the set is more important to you than you are to the set. Thus, as time passes, they will perceive you as having progressively lower value. A high-value male doesn't put himself in uncomfortable situations just so he can seek rapport with others.

Unfortunately, you can't simply approach a seated set and join them at their table. To do so would be try-hard. So what is the field-tested best practice for opening a seated set?

1. Open the set (as you would for a standing set).
2. Part of the way into the opener, use a false time constraint.
3. Continue the opener as you grab a chair and sit down with the set. It's important to be talking at the same time that you sit down.
4. Stack to your next routine, then stand again as if to leave (a nonverbal FTC), while you speak.
5. Sit again as you FTC, then stack.

Knowing the steps is not enough. It takes repeated practice in the field to tighten up your ability to open, false-time-constrain, and stack smoothly. Often it isn't the techniques themselves that matter most but the manner in which they are executed.

Body Language
When you first run your opener, don't face the set with your body. Your head may be turned toward the set as you address them, but the rest of your body should not be.

You can tell a lot just by where someone's feet are pointing. If you come across as *rapport seeking* during the opener, the set will perceive it as a low-value behavior. They will treat you like a low-value guy and blow you out of the set. Field-testing has shown me that the percentage of sets that open successfully is drastically affected by this one factor.

There are two common opening scenarios worth mentioning at this time. In the first, you are simply walking by the set *on your way back to your friends.* As you pass the target set, stop, turn your head toward them, and run your opener. As the opener hooks, you can then turn the rest of your body toward the set.

In the second scenario, you are already in a set, adjacent to the target group. This gives you social proof. At the right time, simply lean back toward the target group and, over your shoulder, run an opener. As before, when they start to hook, you can turn your body toward them.

Calibrate!

Often a girl will turn her body in to face you as she hooks to your material. When she does this, you should then turn your body toward her as well. (Reward her for good behavior.) If you do this prematurely, you will come across as needy or overeager. Feel the calibration *flow*. Within the first thirty to sixty seconds of running the opener, your body should be facing the set—and they should be facing you. You can't run the set over your shoulder, but you should open it that way.

Lean Back

The next time you are in the field, observe various conversations. Notice how one person may lean in, while another leans back. The person leaning back will appear to hold more power than the person leaning in. When you lean in, you convey that your target is more important to you than you are to her. This reveals that you have lower value than she does. A subtlety like this is often the critical factor in losing a set. In fact, many beginners engage in **pecking,** which is the act of leaning in every time they say something. Do not do this! The woman's emotional circuitry will inform her that you are not a man of high survival and replication value, and she will stop responding to you.

Tonality and Pacing

The quality of your voice is extremely important. Although no problem is insurmountable, certain vocal qualities are preferable to others. Some important points:

+ **Have a deep, powerful voice that comes from your diaphragm:** If you have any issues with an accent that is considered unattractive—you know who you are—get a voice coach and have the problem fixed.

+ **Be emotionally expressive with your voice:** It may be useful to take classes on acting and improvisational comedy.
+ **Speak slowly and clearly:** Eliminate "uh," "like," and "you know" from your vocabulary.
+ **Speak. With plenty. Of pausing:** Create . . . a certain rhythm . . . to the way . . . that you speak. This will rivet attention to your words.
+ **Speak loudly:** Women are programmed to respond automatically to a man with a louder voice. This doesn't mean that you should lack social discretion and talk loudly all the time. But recognize that it is a useful tool at your disposal, especially in louder venues. This will make you come across as "more alpha."

These are all very easy to field-test. Open ten sets with a loud voice, using plenty of pausing, and then open ten sets with a quiet voice without pausing. The difference in response is striking. *The field does not lie.*

Incongruence

Have you ever tried to use another person's personality-conveying routine, only to have it come out of your mouth like a bad script? When what you say and how you say it don't match up in a natural manner you have what Venusian artists call **incongruence.**

To get a woman interested in you, you must be interesting. That is why Venusian artists share stories and trade gambits. **What one man can do, another man can do.** Some have suggested that you should "just be yourself" and not use interesting, field-tested, proven material. But this material creates the opportunity to get valuable practice in the field, building calibration. What's more, it gives you something interesting to say.

Like a comedian, a pickup artist is also a performing artist. A pickup artist's task is to captivate a small group of people long enough to convey specific personality characteristics that ultimately make him interesting to the one woman in the group whom he has his eye on.

The material he runs is the vehicle with which he conveys his personality to the group—and, obliquely, to her. When a comedian tells a joke, people say, "That's funny." But when he strings several good jokes together, people say, "*He's* hilarious." It is no longer the material that receives the acclaim but the comedian himself.

Picture this: An amateur comedian is hanging out with friends and accidentally tells a funny joke during conversation, generating a great response. He thinks to himself, *Man, that was funny. I'm going to put that in my comedy act.* So a few days later, he does—only the comedy routine falls flat. He thinks to himself, *When I said it to my friends, they really cracked up. It must be the audience.*

So the next week he throws the joke into his act again, and again it fails to make the audience laugh. He thinks, *Hmm, why didn't this work? Is it the material or the audience that's to blame?*

He decides to try the material out one more time the following week, and again the routine fails to make people laugh. He's had enough—he drops the routine entirely.

Now let's look at what a professional comedian does. You see, it is the professional who knows that reciting a joke only three times in front of an audience is simply not enough practice. He knows he must tell the joke again and again in front of a live audience to systematically reconstruct the natural timing that the joke had the first time he told it to his friends.

The bad news is that every new routine that you learn must go through this **naturalization phase.** In fact, it may take a good two dozen tries until the scripted routine comes out congruently. The good news is, when you're doing a dozen approaches a night, you'll have a totally natural routine in the can in only two nights. And if you add a new routine to your game on a weekly basis, you'll soon have a whole list of routines in the can when you really need them.

There will come a time in your near future that you will be given an opportunity to attract a woman of particular quality. Are you ready for the challenge? Meaning, do you have enough material naturalized and ready to go, so you can attract her with congruence?

SOCIAL PROOF

Some players may be seen walking around a venue, eyeballing all the women and looking for a good one to approach. This behavior looks predatory and is quite transparent to others in the crowd. Walk around alone long enough and women will assume you have no "alignments." It takes only minutes to rupture your social value.

Other guys may be seen standing in a group and looking around. If they don't look like they belong, aren't hanging out with girls, or aren't running a set, they will demonstrate a lower social value than those who do or are. When one of them finally does open a set, he may discover that opening is more difficult in environments where he now has **negative social proof.**

The Venusian artist, rolling in with his pivot or wing, will not look around at all the people in the crowd. Rather, he'll talk to his friend, and it will appear that they are two high-value people enjoying each other's company.

If he *were* to look around the venue, especially with a serious expression on his face, he would telegraph to others that he was looking for something with more value than the spot where he already stood. A good pickup artist believes that the most fun and valuable spot in the field is his own.

Women are searching for a man whose reality is more fun and valuable than their own. You must be congruent with the value that you have to offer, and it must be apparent to the room, revealed through a series of distinct demonstrations of high social value. Follow the Three-Second Rule, and you will be in set much more often, resulting in higher social proof.

Whenever you have higher social proof, you will get noticeably more occurrences of proximity. Girls will also give you other **approach invitations,** such as making eye contact. It's not necessarily desirable to wait around for such approach invitations, however. With practice, a Venusian artist can regularly open sets without them.

REVIEW

+ A1 begins when you run an opener.
+ A1 is complete when you reach the **social hook point.** This is the moment when the set ceases to wonder when you will leave and instead hopes that you will stay.
+ The **meeting location** is a **target-rich** environment that the Venusian artist visits in order to practice his game. This is also known as a **field.**
+ Women will often use **proximity** to signal their receptiveness to an approach. They may not be consciously aware they are doing this.
+ Although proximity and other **approach invitations** are opportunities to be capitalized on, a skilled pickup artist can consistently open sets without waiting for these signals.
+ The **Three-Second Rule** states that upon entering the field, you must open a set within three seconds. Also, if you are later not in a set and you see one, then you must open it within three seconds. Following this rule will give you higher **social proof,** which affects how people respond to you.
+ The Mystery Method makes use of **indirect openers** because they do not telegraph interest and are proven in the field to open consistently. Other types of openers can also be quite effective, such as direct openers. Experiment and field-test your ideas.
+ Don't try to look "cool" or "tough." It's better to be comfortable and friendly.
+ It's normal to need two or three **warm-up approaches** at the beginning of the night.

- ✦ Don't drink.
- ✦ Try to approach sets that include men, and practice gaming them as well. **Women have a "leader-of-men" attraction switch.**
- ✦ Women have various **protection shield strategies,** which they use to screen out men. But a Venusian artist can coax a woman into lowering her shield by **conveying lack of interest** while **demonstrating value.**
- ✦ The Mystery Method makes use of **canned material,** which can generate consistent responses. You should create a **routine stack** in order to practice this skill.
- ✦ The natural delivery of the material, including body language, facial expressions, and vocal tonality, is more important than the content itself.
- ✦ An opener must have situational relevance.
- ✦ A **false time constraint** or FTC allows the Venusian artist to create the illusion that he is about to leave. This is a powerful tool for opening consistently.
- ✦ **Body rocking** is the use of body language to deliver a false time constraint.
- ✦ When you are opening a moving set, it is important that they not perceive you as chasing them in any way.
- ✦ When opening a seated set, it is important to sit with them soon after starting the opener. **Use a false time constraint and then continue talking as you sit down.**
- ✦ The use of new material in the field can feel clumsy and **incongruent.** Only through several days of in-field practice can the new material become naturalized.
- ✦ You can create **negative social proof** with certain behaviors, such as standing against the wall with your drink against your chest, standing in a group of guys, circling the venue in a predatory fashion, looking around the venue with a serious expression on your face, et cetera.

6.

A2: FEMALE-TO-MALE INTEREST

Demonstrating value, indicators of interest, and group theory

Now that the set is open, it's time to create attraction. First, you must pick a target from the set. Maybe there are several pretty girls and your decision is somewhat arbitrary, but you still must choose one so that you can **neg** her. If you aren't physically attracted to any of them, choose an **arbitrary target** just for practice. You'll make new friends.

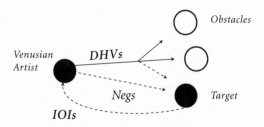

As you **demonstrate higher value** (DHV) to the set and neg the target, attraction is created. She will respond with IOIs, which will help you to gauge your progress. This is the essence of the A2 phase.

IOIS

As discussed earlier, when a girl feels attracted to someone, she will begin to reveal subtle but distinct indicators of interest. Spotting these as they stream out of her helps us gauge her internal state. A woman may deliberately give you these indicators, but often they are not conscious. Often men, Venusian artists included, also give IOIs unconsciously. With practice, we become desensitized to the presence of beautiful women and avoid this problem.

Here are examples of IOIs. Notice that some of these require more attraction than others. For example, a woman might be attracted enough to ask you your name but not enough to leave the venue with you and bounce.

- She reinitiates conversation when you stop talking.
- She giggles.
- She touches you.
- She tries to get rapport and build comfort with you.
- She looks back and glances at you repeatedly every minute or so.
- She tosses her hair (to see if you will look).
- If eye contact happens from a distance, she holds it for a second.
- She smiles at you.
- She stands nearby (proximity).
- She interrupts your conversation from nearby or laughs at something you said.
- While walking by, she turns her body toward you or brushes against you.
- She says something to her friend and they both giggle.
- She asks you for a light or the time or in any way initiates a conversation.
- While you're talking to her group, she is particularly talkative (to get your attention).
- She asks you for your name.
- She asks you your age. (Make her guess.)

+ She compliments you.
+ She is playful and tries to challenge you.
+ She's disagreeing but laughing.
+ She's punching your arm but laughing.
+ She uses nicknames for you.
+ She plays with her hair while talking to you.
+ When she is sitting next to you her leg touches yours.
+ She repeatedly touches you in any way.
+ She asks if you have a girlfriend.
+ She mentions your girlfriend without knowing if you actually have one.
+ When she has to go to the bathroom, she comes back.
+ She holds eye contact for longer periods of time when she speaks with you.
+ She avoids mentioning her boyfriend.
+ If it comes up that you like something, she mentions that she likes it, too, or needs someone to show her how to do it.
+ When she says or does something, she looks at you to see your reaction.
+ She looks at you from the side, to hide the fact that she's looking.
+ She introduces you to friends.
+ She buys you a drink.
+ She calls you a player or a heartbreaker.
+ On her way out, she reapproaches to tell you that she is leaving. (Get her number.)
+ On your way out, she asks you where you are going. (Invite her.)
+ She returns your calls.
+ She invents reasons to be near you, interact with you, or have isolation with you.

The most important IOIs to look for are:

+ She reinitiates conversation when you stop talking.
+ She giggles.

* She touches you.
* She tries to get rapport and build comfort with you.

Sometimes it isn't when she *does* something but rather when she *doesn't* do something that she's expressing interest. These are called **passive IOIs,** and they're very important because often they're the only IOIs you'll get. Here are a few examples:

* Her friends go (to the bathroom or bar or dancing), but she stays.
* She comes to see you and hangs with you for extended periods.
* If you move, she follows you or waits for you.
* She doesn't flinch or pull back if you happen to get too close.
* She doesn't resist when you escalate physically (or she gives token resistance to avoid feeling like a slut).

Fake IOIs

Be warned that girls may fake IOIs and lie to you. For example, a girl might give you IOIs while she is asking you to buy her a drink. She's not attracted to you but merely manipulating you. And, of course, if you are easily manipulated, she will find you less attractive. She might give you IOIs just to keep you around as free entertainment.

A girl also might give IOIs when she is in fact ditching you. For example, when she says, "We have to go to the bathroom now," if in the back of her mind she knows she is really ditching you, she might touch you on the arm as she says good-bye, to give you some validation.

A girl will also sometimes give IOIs just to see if she can get you to return them. If you return her IOIs too easily, without making her work for it, you have just become another notch on her validation belt and she may pursue greater challenges elsewhere. Don't jump on her just because she compliments you.

INDICATORS OF DISINTEREST (IODS)

Similarly, there are IODs. Here are a few examples of these:

+ Avoidance: She avoids eye contact. She avoids your calls. She avoids you in general.
+ If she can pretend that she didn't hear what you just said, she will.
+ She won't contribute to the conversation.
+ She gets impatient easily.
+ She walks away or looks away.
+ She leans away, turns her back, or talks to someone else.
+ She is nonresponsive, or she repetitively says "uh-huh" instead of giving you a real response.
+ She won't move with you, even two feet away. She won't invest.

Practicing A1 and A2 will develop the skill set to get IOIs instead of IODs. The path to mastery is not found by telling a hot woman that she is hot, offering to buy her a drink, being too persistent, or asking her lots of questions. Instead, practice A1 (be indirect and nonneedy) and practice A2 (stagger "negs" with demonstrations of higher value). Voilà! IOIs.

For those who have seen the movie *The Tao of Steve,* A1 and A2 correspond to the first two rules in the movie: *be desireless* and *be excellent.*

NEG THEORY

Beautiful women (9s and 10s) endure a daily stream of awkward moments when otherwise harmless guys say, "Where are you from?" "What's *your* name?" and, "You're beautiful." Many women have developed the ability to make these guys go away by being a bitch, and it works. Are beautiful women really bitches? Doubtful. The truth is, many of my girlfriends were both beautiful and warm . . . once I worked through their initial defenses with the judicious use of negs.

If a woman doesn't develop strategies for quickly dismissing this daily barrage of bore, she'll find herself trapped in conversations with just about anyone, even those with little survival and replication value. After all, until you DHV, you can't expect a girl to feel you have any value anyway. Remember, you must first create a social opportunity to DHV before judgment can be made by your target.

Women who are 9s and 10s find themselves saying no to men with such regularity that when they finally meet a man who has legitimate value for them, they may, on reflex, respond abrasively. There is a silver lining to this dark cloud, however: Hot women say no so often that when they do meet someone they deem to have high value, yes means, *Yes! Finally!*

In today's social environment, beautiful women have to become very good at brushing off men. After all, they're not going to sleep with every one of the men. They may say no, act annoyed, or use some other shielding mechanism. Many poor guys are left walking off angry and feeling like a failure, thinking a woman is a bitch for rejecting them harshly.

If a woman accepts a beer from you when you have just met, the underlying social dynamic translates to, "I don't know you, and I don't care about you. You are just another one of those typical guys and since I don't respect you, I'll take that beer before I snub you."

Her train of thought reads, *If the guys are stupid enough to buy me drinks, I'm smart enough to take them.*

Hot girls are good at snubbing your approach. You will have to learn how to snub them back. Now that doesn't mean you should insult them. They are accustomed to the men they've hurt saying, "You are nothing but a bitch!"

So how do you snub a hot girl back without insulting her?

Let's imagine for a moment that a girl has long nails, which in today's society are often acrylic. The Venusian artist approaches and says, "Nice nails. Are they real?" She will have to concede they aren't. Like he didn't notice the question was a put-down, he says, "Oh [Pause.] Well, I guess they still look good." He then casually turns his back to her for a moment.

What does this do to her? Immediately she will feel like she just lost value in his eyes. But he didn't treat her like shit by insulting her. That only would have made her defend herself with more snubs or walk away. Instead, he complimented her, but the result was to target her insecurity. Her train of thought reads, *I'm beautiful . . . but I didn't win this guy over. Why not? I'm so good at this. I'll just fix his perception of me. Everyone wants me.*

He continues to show a lack of interest in her looks and initiates a neutral topic. During this time, her intention is to get him to conform so she can feel in control. Once revalidated, she can shut him down and move on. Before this can happen, though, he gives her another neg. "Is that a hairpiece? Well, it's nice. This hairstyle should be called the Waffle." He smiles playfully and stacks to another routine.

He is pleasant but uninterested in her beauty. This intrigues her because she knows how most men behave and this isn't normal for her. This man must be used to girls, or married (preselected), or *something*. These questions make her curious. She gives him little negs, which she uses to test for congruence. He passes these by lightly negging her back.

He pauses in a story to say, "Ah, that's so funny! Your nose wiggles when you speak. Look, there it goes again. Ha!" She blushes.

Now she is self-conscious—and this is where he wants her. He has, with only three negs, successfully created interest and removed her from her pedestal, thereby circumventing her protection shield and buying himself more time to DHV.

✦ NEG:

[Canadian] Verb, noun: a statement or action made to briefly and without insult disqualify oneself from being perceived as a potential suitor.
Usage: to neg someone, to be negged, to throw negs, to master negging.

A neg is not an insult but a negative social value judgment that is telegraphed. It's the same as if you pulled out a tissue and blew your nose. There's nothing insulting about blowing your nose. You haven't explicitly rejected her. But at the same time, she will feel that you aren't even trying to impress her. This makes her curious as to why and makes you a challenge. Examples: "Too bad I'm gay," "Where's your off button?" "No touchy," "I've eaten girls like you for breakfast."

Generally, I found the better looking the woman, the more aggressive your negs will need to be. A 10 may get three negs up front in quick succession just for being beautiful, while an 8 gets only one or two. You can go overboard if she thinks *you think* you are better than her (which happens more often that you'd expect). Not only is it cruel to drop a woman's self-esteem out from under her (regardless of the fact that most 10s will readily do this to guys), but not-too-surprisingly, it doesn't get you the girl. Get as close to the breaking point as you can without crossing the line. When you reach the point where she is about to retaliate, start appreciating things about her (but not her looks). Mutual respect has formed, and respect is something men rarely get from a girl in the field.

If you do accidentally offend her completely and she complains about your behavior (this isn't recommended, but it also doesn't necessarily preclude you from mating), allow her to vent her emotions by voicing her opinion of you entirely first. Then say, "I'm monumentally sorry. I didn't mean to step over your boundaries. I merely intended to find them. Now that I know where they are, I promise . . . I will not cross them again. I'm sorry." From there, the Game is on.

Hot girls can be opened with a neg. Pepper three of them into two to three minutes of neutral chat, and once the protection shield is removed, you can, from a place of mutual respect, built comfort with the girl.

Here are some examples of effective negs:

+ **Mystery:** I don't think we should get to know each other.
  Girl: Why not?
  Mystery: You're just too much of a nice girl for me.

+ If your target says something rude, say, "You don't get out much, do you?"
+ If your target interrupts you, say, "Hello, I'm talking, jeez," or, "Excuse me . . . may I finish my sentence first?" You then say to others in the group, "Is she always like that?" and roll your eyes playfully.
+ If you are asking a question to two women and the target answers, you say, "I didn't ask you."
+ If you pull out your photos for the **photo routine,** first show them to the obstacle. When the target tries to see them, say, "Excuse me! I'm showing *her* the pictures, not *you.* Wait your turn, jeez."
+ If a girl kisses you on the cheek and goes to kiss your other cheek, tell her, "Only one . . . don't be greedy." If she says, "Yes, but I'm French," you reply, "Are all French girls as greedy as you?"
+ "That's a nice hairstyle . . . is that your real hair?" Smile and look at her to show her you are being sincere and not insulting.

+ **Her:** *Oh, I'm a model.*
  You: *What, like a hand model?*

+ *"Ewww, your palms are sweaty . . . ewwww!!!!! Where have your hands been? No, don't tell me; I do not want to know!"*
+ "You've got something in your ear."

+ **You:** *Watch this. Here, pull my finger. This is good. [Your target pulls your finger. Make a fart sound with your lips.] Wow. You actually pulled my finger! Haaa! No, no jus' kidding, here, really, pull on my finger. No, honest, this is good; trust me. [She pulls it—fart sound again.] Oh man!!! That's twice!!! I can't believe you! My niece is six and doesn't fall for that shit anymore! How old are you?*

You may decide to say, "I'm just kidding. Here *really.* I'll show you some magic. Look at this. My hand is empty right? OK, really pull my finger. No, really, I promise I won't fart again. Serious. I swear to you. Magician's honor! No, swear. I promise I won't. [She pulls your finger. Fart sound] Oh my God, you can get talked into *anything!*

+ "I like that dress. I remember seeing you at a club before and you were wearing the same dress. It *is* nice though."

+ "My, you come on strong. That isn't 'til later in the relationship."

+ "Very good. That is a little test I do to see if you have any free thoughts of your own or just believe everything you hear."

+ "Wow. You really wrecked a moment! Your ex-boyfriends must have really hated that about you."

+ **Her:** *I'm a model.*
  You: *Do a lot of people ask you if you are a model?*
  Her: *Yes, all the time.*
  You: *I think they were just being polite.*

+ "I just noticed . . . your nose wiggles when you speak . . . haa, it's so cute." Point and say, "Look, there it goes again; you're like Samantha from *Bewitched* . . . but only when you speak."

+ **You:** *[Take a stick of gum out and offer it to the target.]*
  Her: *No thanks. I'm drinking beer.*
  You: *I know. Take the gum.*

If She's Older:

+ If your target says, "You are so young," this is an IOI. Don't excuse yourself for being young like chumps do—only someone trying to get the girl would do that. Simply reply cynically, "Yeah, I noticed . . . poor you." Remember to convey your playful teasing attitude.

+ "Take a quiet moment to get over this age thing. I'll wait."

TYPES OF NEGS

Shotgun Neg

These are statements such as, "Wow, she poops words." And, "Where's her off button?" You can use these on the target in a group to convey lack of interest romantically. A neg is in fact an IOD. Of course, it's not that you *dislike* her—not at all. It's just that you hadn't considered her a romantic interest. This IOD diminishes her sexual power over you, while simultaneously disarming her peer group. The shotgun neg is a great social tool, said for the group's benefit. It keeps her friends from thinking you have a sexual motive, and that keeps them from protecting her from you. The power of the shotgun neg is in its apparent sincerity. She'll honestly believe that you aren't trying to impress her. Then she'll wonder . . . *why*.

Shotgun negs are useful for conveying a *nonneedy* attitude—which is a demonstration of higher value. Thus in one stroke you indicate lack of interest, disarm obstacles, and create attraction.

Tease Neg

Teasing conveys a cocky, playful attitude. It's not perceived as inadvertent but rather as deliberate flirting (but done properly). Examples of this are, "Pull my finger . . . phft! Wow, you fell for it. Weirdo," "You can dress her up, but you can't take her anywhere," "Don't make me come down there," etc. When you call her a knucklehead, your cocky, playful, fun attitude reveals you are confident, unaffected, and in control. Teasing stimulates her emotions and is useful as a DHV during A2. It is directed to either the group as a whole or the target directly.

Sniper Neg

A sniper neg is used directly on the target and she is the only one to hear it. Some examples of this are hinting to her that she should immediately wipe her nose, has a crusty eye, has sweaty palms, or just spat on you while talking . . . and it actually grossed you out. The idea is to make her honestly believe that she has performed a **demonstration of** lower value (DLV). This makes her self-conscious and creates a situation where *she* is wondering whether you have a good impression of her.

You can follow a sniper neg up by looking away or dropping the conversation for a moment or some other IOD. Why? *Her embarrassment makes her vulnerable to later flattery.* By indicating even a slight lack of interest using subtleties in your body language, you can create in her a powerful desire to win your approval and validation.

The Throw and Go Rule

Toss your neg like a pebble. Before it reaches its destination, turn your head away and continue the conversation with the group in a "throw and go" fashion. As far as she can tell, it's not something that you're still thinking about or gave much thought to in the first place.

As you weave together the multiple threads of your conversation, occasionally the time will come to calibrate and throw a neg. When this happens, it's important that your target doesn't see you watching for her reaction. If you are trying to get a reaction out of her, **she won't perceive the neg as genuine and inadvertent, and thus it won't work.** Furthermore, reaction-seeking behavior is a DLV.

DHV

Anything you can do that conveys higher S-and-R value is a **DHV.** For example, if you open a set and already have two girls with you, you have demonstrated preselection, which is a DHV. When girls see that other girls have preselected you, they feel attracted to you as a result.

If a woman discovers that you have a lot of money, it is a DHV. A rich man may mean a rich lifestyle for her, and she is hardwired to improve her chances of survival and replication by aligning with those who *can* help her. She will find you more attractive. If she perceives that you are *trying to impress her* with your money, though, she will then *lose* attraction. This is because only lower-value people try to impress—such behavior is considered DLV. If you are trying to impress, you must be of lower status and thus unattractive.

If a woman sees that you have a lot of social proof from gaming the room, *she will feel more attracted to you.* Social proof is a DHV. If, however, she sees that you are socially unaware and inept, then it is a DLV. When you DLV, it lowers her perception of your S-and-R value, which makes her feel emotionally less attracted.

Telling stories that are fun, interesting and emotionally relevant demonstrates social skill, which is a DHV. A story can also be structured to convey specific characteristics in the *subtext,* allowing you to surreptitiously flip attraction switches.

Negging is also a DHV, because only a high-value male would talk to her like that, and seem sincerely uninterested.

Examples of DHVs:

+ Preselection from other women
+ Appearing to be a leader of men
+ Being supporter and protector of those you love
+ Being nonneedy
+ Being unaffected
+ Social intelligence
+ Negging her (this IOD is a DHV also)
+ Having a strong frame
+ Having interesting knowledge
+ Emotional stimulation
+ Being socially "in demand"—other people are seeking your attention or validation (alternately *they* are paying attention to what *you* are saying)
+ Connecting conversationally

GROUP THEORY

Women of quality tend to be found in groups and rarely, if ever, alone. When girls get together, they engage in a *groupthink* mentality. This groupthink is due to the same psychological mechanism that causes preselection: Girls look to one another to validate their choices and feelings. They will touch one another, hold hands, whisper things,

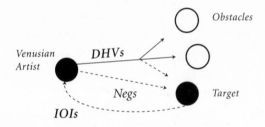

move around the venue together, go to the bathroom together, rescue one another from aggressive guys or nice-guy losers, and generally take care of one another.

Often the nice guy waits for the girl to leave her group so that he can catch her alone and hit on her. But in the Mystery Method, we approach the group itself. Women tend to be attracted to the highest-value man in their social context. **Could it be possible to take over her group and become the highest-value man in it?**

Once the set is open, you disarm the friends with stories, humor, and other DHVs. You're interesting, fun, and emotionally relevant. In fact, you even steal the spotlight away from the hottie (who is the target).

You further disarm the friends by negging the target. All those other predatory guys tried to open by giving her IOIs and offering to buy her a drink—they are so transparent. But you negged her, turned your back, and continued telling your story. The friends don't perceive any threat, as you demonstrated a noninsulting indicator of lack of interest—they're **disarmed.** Unbeknownst to them, the negs have also introduced a tasty sexual tension between you and the target.

Because her friends love you, her groupthink mentality now works in your favor. You have the social proof of her peer group. Her self-esteem has been lowered slightly by the negs, and she wants some more attention from you—the life of the party, the guy who just pushed her out of the spotlight of her own circle of friends. She begins to give you IOIs, and she begins to work for your approval and validation. If you can consistently create reactions like this, you have mastered A2.

Basic group theory operates on a combination of two DHVs:

* ESP and its possibility or impossibility
* How you met a bear while hiking
* How you were scared shitless rock climbing when your rope snapped
* The time you accompanied your friend to visit a girl and your buddy was almost beaten to death when the girl he visited had a boyfriend who came out and there was a twenty-minute car chase through lights and you were looking for the cops but lost the crazed boyfriend before you found any
* The time you were in the hospital and it changed the way food tastes or the way birds sound clearer now
* The time you hacked into a bank but chickened out and put the money into a charity
* The time you lived with four girls and when they all had PMS there was a giant food fight
* The famous person you met
* Whether she believes in ghosts and why or why not
* You like candles and incense; what does *she* like?
* The ant farm you bought for your niece and what you learned from the experience
* The time you were onstage
* The time you bladed down a steep hill and survived

1. The social proof that is generated by taking over the group. Personality traits are also demonstrated to the group and thus, obliquely, to the target.
2. The ability of the neg not only to convey higher value but also to simultaneously disarm the obstacles, remove the target's sexual power, and motivate her to chase you to get it back.

MULTIPLE CONVERSATIONAL THREADS

During a conversation, especially between people who are already acquainted with one another, various conversational threads will come up. We might talk about the weather, our families, what we did last night, various philosophical topics or current events, etc. As the conversation progresses, certain threads may be revisited or come up periodically.

People who are not as well acquainted, however, often find comfort in a thread that has situational relevance and end up stuck on that one thread until it eventually unravels. Imagine a guy is walking his dog in the park and he meets a woman doing the same. They strike up a conversation:

Man: *Oh, hello, is that a cocker spaniel?*
Woman: *No, actually, he's a mutt. I got him from the pound a few years ago. How about yours?*
Man: *She's a black Lab. I suppose they are getting on rather well then, aren't they?*
Woman: *Yes, yes, they are; dogs are funny.*
Man: *So have you had him for long?*
Woman: *Oh, I don't know, about three years.*
Man: *So . . . so what sort of dog food do you feed him?*

Notice how the man is already grasping for straws? He was successfully interacting with the woman on this dog thread, but he couldn't think of another thread with situational relevance in order to continue the conversation. So he went back to the dog thread again, making it rather obvious that the conversation with the woman was important to him, that he didn't want to "screw this up." This is especially telegraphed by his overuse of questions during conversation as well.

People who are well acquainted with one another tend to use multiple conversational threads while talking, whereas people who aren't as well acquainted can get stuck on a single thread, followed by a polite end to the conversation:

Man: *Do you have the time?*
Woman: *Sure, six thirty.*
Man: *Thanks. So, where are you from?*

If you go further by starting a new thread rather than continuing with a previously opened and paused thread, you telegraph interest and force her to decide prematurely whether or not to bust out her protection shield kung-fu "I have a boyfriend" objection.

By introducing multiple conversational threads into your set, you can create a strong feeling of familiarity in the set, as if you are already all old friends.

In the early part of a set, when you haven't yet demonstrated much value, girls won't be eager to contribute much effort to continue the interaction. You must be able to contribute 90 percent of the conversation or it will die.

Over time, as attraction is created, you can then use this at-

Elvis Gambit

"Hey, did you know that Elvis Presley dyed . . . his hair? What was his original hair color? Guess. . . . No, dirty blond. Can you picture the King as a Beach Boy blond? He would never have been famous if he didn't go 'bad boy' and dye his hair black. Weird."

traction to bait the girl into more participation and investment. But even then you must be leading the interaction and keeping her stimulated. Thus it's extremely important that you be able to **talk talk talk.**

Always have something to talk about. Get into a talkative mood and practice talking to everyone, not just hot girls. Introduce several different routines and jump back and forth between them in a multiple threading fashion instead of running them linearly.

Notice how logistical problems seem to disappear when you keep the target's conscious mind occupied with three to five simultaneous conversational threads. You've always got a thread to go back to, whereas your set can sour quickly when there are too many uncomfortable pauses or if it suddenly appears like you are grasping at straws to keep the interaction alive.

CUTTING CONVERSATIONAL THREADS

Sometimes a thread is not useful. A girl may start talking about something that makes her feel bored or sad or think about her boyfriend back home, et cetera. For whatever reason, it is more useful to you to end that conversational topic than to continue talking about it. When this happens, simply CUT the thread and stack to the next routine.

Her: . . . *So every time I hear that song, I think of him.*
You: *Let me see your hands. [Begin the kino (kinesthetic) test.]*

Just completely cut her thread and replace it with a new thread of your own. Of course this doesn't mean that you need to become Mr. Interrupt, who refuses to address every issue. Just recognize that when it is useful to you, you can cut a thread, introduce a new thread to replace it, and still stay on track. In fact, not only will it work, but also she will find you more attractive as a result, since it demonstrates that you have a stronger **frame.**

Sometimes it can happen that one of your own threads is not useful anymore. For example, if one of her friends has just joined the set in the middle of your thread, this can be awkward. If you finish the story, the friend will be bored because she has no idea what you're talking about. But if you start over from the beginning, now the target is bored because she has already heard this before, and by the time you get to the end it has become anticlimactic.

To handle this external interrupt, just cut your own thread, disarm the obstacle with a target-bound neg, and introduce a new thread:

You: . . . *So I'm halfway back to the house, and there's only three minutes left, and I notice the can is starting to leak—*
[Her friend arrives and the girls immediately face each other and start signaling each other.]
You: *Introduce me to your friend, that's the polite thing to do.*
[Brief introductions occur. As you shake her hand, shotgun neg the target one more time to disarm new obstacle.]
You: [new thread addressed to the friend] *Do you believe in spells? OK, get this.* . . . [Spells routine.]

Oh, and don't try to go back to your original thread later, unless they press for you to do so. It's try-hard.

Often, if you do not lead the conversation by actively cutting bad threads and introducing good threads, you delegate this responsibility to the girl. She will allow the conversation to get boring and then think that you are a boring guy for allowing it to happen. So do it right and make it happen, because *she won't.*

The Waypoint

The line "So how do you all know each other?" is a question that must be asked in *every* set at some point. Take a moment and recite it a few times. Get used to the statement, because you will be repeating it often.

It seems like a harmless, reasonable, sociable question, but it generates conversation *and* provides the Venusian artist with useful information. For example, if the set consists of two girls and you ask, "So how do you guys know each other?" it's possible that one of them will say, "Oh, she's my boyfriend's sister." Would this new information possibly change your game plan? I wager so.

The important information isn't the existence of a boyfriend. If your game is tight, girls will secretly cheat on their boyfriends without even telling you that he exists. Rather, the important information is that she is probably not going to cheat on her boyfriend *in front of his sister,* who is standing right here.

"So how do you all know each other?" might also reveal that the group consists of co-workers, or that the guy you thought was a threat was actually your target's brother. (Lucky you were doing the Mystery Method and befriended him with DHV routines before conveying IOIs to his sister.)

The moment when you ask this question is the **waypoint** of the set, and it typically occurs three to five minutes in.

WINGING

The Wing Rules

1. **He who opens the set leads the set:** He gets first choice of target. Your wing may open for you.

2. **Make your primary purpose as wing to help the pickup artist get his target:** If you can also game up your own target from the group, fine. But that is not your first priority.

3. **Don't jack the set:** Don't ever steal your wing's target. Sometimes the player is ignoring or negging his target while working the group. It would be really easy to go into his set at this point and give attention to the target—don't.

4. **Remember that if the player cannot advance in any way** in the set due to kino lockout, Let's Just Be Friends (LJBF), or a general lack of IOIs, **the wing may then attempt to recover the set for himself. Debate who decides before you are infield.**

5. **As a wing, occupy the obstacles** so that the player gets more time one-on-one with his target.

6. **Always agree with your wing:** Never take the girls' side over his. He is always right.

7. **Remember your wing is a great guy, a cool guy:** That is why you hang out with him. After all, you have high standards.

8. **Keep in mind that your wing's feelings are important to you, even more important than the girl's feelings.** If he approaches your set, you will turn to face him. (Girls do the same with their friends.) If you disrespect your wing, it will lower *your* value to the girls! Never leave him standing around without acknowledging him or introducing him.

Entering a Set As a Wing
THE "WERE YOU GUYS JUST TALKING ABOUT . . ." GAMBIT

1. The player has opened a set and has had enough time to pass the social hook point, usually within three minutes. The wing approaches the player.

2. Player faces wing and greets him.

3. Player then says, "Hey, guys, this is my friend [name]."

4. Wing says, "Oh, were you guys just talking about . . ."

5. Player says, "Yeah, when that girl cast a spell on Aaron . . ."

Conversation continues from this point. Wing is now in the set.

The Accomplishment Introduction
Get your wing to introduce you by name *and* accomplishment:

✦ "He's the guy who [fill in blank]."
✦ "This is Mystery. He levitated over Niagara Falls."
✦ "I'd like to introduce you to Glen. He's the guy they wrote about who hacked into the power grid and turned off California for six hours."
✦ "He dated Miss November. Beautiful!"

These are **accomplishment introductions.** If *you* talk about yourself, it's like tooting your own horn and is try-hard. But if your wing does it, it's likely to be believed. All you need is some minor proof. An article photocopied to sign for them, a comp card with your picture on it to leave with them, or a photo of you with a beautiful girl in a bikini. (Keep that one for your photo routine.)

Remember, you don't have to *be* what you *do.* You just have to convey an *accomplishment.* Make it bigger than life. You don't have to lie. Make it *true.* Be great.

THE ACCOMPLISHMENT INTRO GAMBIT

1. The player has opened a set and has had enough time to pass the social hook point. The wing approaches the player.
2. Player faces wing and greets him.
3. Player then says, "Hey, guys, this is my friend [name]; he's:
   "making me a very rich man."
   "great people."
   "one of the smartest men I know."
4. Wing says, "Pleasure," then runs the set for a minute.

Conversation continues from this point. Wing is now in the set.

- ✦ "This is Chuck. He's a broker." Boring.
- ✦ "This is Bender. He's the lead singer of this awesome band called Razor. They just got on the charts." Respect.

What is *your* great accomplishment? Write your accomplishment intro for your wing to use. It makes *him* appear cool, too, hanging with a man of accomplishment.

What would you do with your life if you had no chance of failure? What is your dream? What do you honestly want to become? Be great.

It's a powerful dynamic when you and your wing can run stories about each other.

STORYTELLING

When you tell a story, it doesn't have to be overtly impressive. In fact, it's better if it's not some amazing story, because you don't want the target to think you're trying to impress her. As long as the story is fun, interesting, and, most important, captures the attention of her group, it will work. These sorts of stories are most congruent if they are at least partially true and based on events from your own life.

Conveying traits that flip her attraction switches without making it obvious that you're doing so demonstrates higher value and generates attraction. For example, in a story it's possible to flip both the "leader of men" and "protector of loved ones" attraction switches by

> The Gandhi Bit
>
> Did you know Gandhi was a lawyer?
> I did not know this.
> Did you know he lived in England?
> I did not know this.
> Did you know he was hung like a racehorse?
> Mahatma "the Shlong" Gandhi.

congruently adding something like "... so I told him I have no choice, it's my little sister. So he jumps in the car, 'cause you know my friends are there for me one hundred percent and I'm the same way for them; that's just how we are...." The preselection switch and others can be similarly flipped also.

A helpful hint for telling stories in pickup: The shorter the story, the earlier in set you can use it.

Describe in terms of sensation and emotion. When telling stories, men tend to focus on the facts at hand, whereas women look for the sensation and emotion caused by the experience. Structure your language to take this into account. Example:

> **Bad:** This guy grabbed my ass, can you believe that? I looked like an idiot.
> **Good:** Then I felt a strong hand caress my ass and grip it tightly. I turned around, and there was this man with a handlebar mustache smiling suggestively at me. All the girls started laughing. I have never . . . felt so surprised . . . and embarrassed . . . in my entire life!

Notice how this story segment conveys the emotions of surprise and embarrassment, both of which are useful during a story. Three or four story segments like this put together can lead the listener through a little emotional journey. With skilled delivery, this *is* a DHV, even if it doesn't reveal some value-raising factoid about your life.

LOCK-IN PROPS

While you're in the middle of actively ignoring the target by negging her, she could unexpectedly leave the group. To prevent this, you can lock her in using a prop. For example, put your scarf or hat on her. Or hand her your photos (for your *photo routine*) and ask her to hold them for a second. Now you have her **locked in.** At some point in the future, you'll be able to continue interacting with her, even if she temporarily wanders off. This also creates **trust.** By showing that you trust her with your prop—which she could steal—you also build her trust in you.

If she starts to get restless, dangle some bait in the form of a useful statement, such as: "I have something really cool I need to show you in just a sec . . . but before I do . . ." Then stack into another routine.

LOCKING IN

Imagine a two-set is at the bar. They're chatting, surveying the room, and sipping their drinks. (It's not wise to open a set while they are waiting to order drinks—that's a recipe for a constant stream of interrupts in A1 and A2. Wait until the drinks are paid for and served.)

When you open this set, the girls will have their backs to the bar. They will see the entire room behind you, over your shoulder. But you will see nothing except the bar behind them. There is a slight power differential in your positions. As long as they are comfortable in their spots at the bar, with a superior line of sight, and you are slightly less comfortable standing before them, there will be a leak of social power from you to the set.

In other words, you want to take their spot at the bar.

The Spin Maneuver, Adapted to Steal Her Spot

I tell a girl, "Go like this." I hold my hand out at chest level, palm down. Does she comply? If so, I can prepare to guide her to where I want her to stand.

This is a compliance test. If she defies the test and refuses to cooperate, I didn't have enough interest. In which case, I do an IOD, then another DHV, and then offer another compliance test. As I raise her **compliance threshold** using this process of compliance momentum, I can return to this hand-holding "lock-in" maneuver, which she will now comply with, and continue from there.

If she complies, she will hold her hand out to match mine. I take it and say, "Now do a little spin." **This is another compliance test.**

If she complies, I spin her around. During this, **I move her body away from the bar, stepping into her former spot.** Now I am leaning against the bar in the power position instead of her, and she is facing me with her back to the room. Not only does it look like I'm with her group and she's gaming me, but the distraction of the crowd around is minimized. The show is on me now.

I say, "Yeah! That's your reward. And this is the payment . . . ooohhhh!"

like I just playfully punked her by stealing her chair. She totally fell for it. If I've done it artfully, she'll laugh and punch my arm.

I then run another routine to keep her logical mind occupied while continuing to stimulate her and her group (A2).

Once you've locked yourself into the set, the perception in the room will shift 180 degrees. Now the *girls* seem to be all up on *you,* instead of the other way around. Instead of merely talking to the girls, it looks like you *lead* them. This psychology also affects the girls themselves. Soon you are leaning back against the bar comfortably and your target is standing between your legs while you run a kino test.

During A3, always lock into your set at some point, usually three to five minutes into the set. In this example, lean back against something while the girls face you with their backs to the room, or sit comfortably among them. If it looks like you are gaming them instead of the other way around, you're not locked in yet. The whole room should see you comfortably centered within the group. Adjacent sets will perceive you to have high social value.

ROLE-PLAYING

Playful role-playing builds attraction. Invent some absurd scenario in your head and describe it to the woman. Make sure it's fun and playful, not heavy:

Venusian Artist: *You know what I wanna do? . . . You and I are gonna go to Greece . . . and I'll dress you up in a toga and we'll sell hot dogs at the beach. You run the stand. I'll supervise.*

Sometimes little bits of material like this are preferable to longer stories. Practice having normal conversations but then peppering in little bits such as these. Not only is this useful as an attraction tool, but in the comfort phase you may also create a feeling of shared conspiracy:

Venusian Artist: *You know what I wanna do with you? I want us to go to the beach together . . . and you'll wear a nun's outfit and I'll wear a priest's outfit . . . and we'll hold hands and make out in front of everybody.*

FALSE DISQUALIFIERS

Using **false disqualifiers** has a disarming effect while demonstrating value. In fact, false disqualifiers are identical to negs in this regard. These lines demonstrate confidence, fun, a lack of neediness, and a discriminating attitude that says, "I'm the one controlling the situation, I'm the one who is the prize, and I'm the one who is screening you to determine whether or not you qualify for my attention."

Examples:

+ "It would never work out between us."
+ "I can already tell, you and I are *not* going to get along."
+ "You're fired."
+ "You're too much of a nice girl for me."
+ "You're a nurse? Oh my God, I can't even talk to you."
+ "I'm totally not boyfriend material. Hey, that guy over there looks *perfect* for you."
+ "We are so broken up. I want my CDs back."

If you think telling a girl that you and she would never get along in order to attract her ultimately is counterintuitive, I agree, wholeheartedly. Disqualify yourself from being a potential suitor, *then* DHV. With experience, these challenging IODs can be powerfully persuasive.

THE PHOTOGRAPHIC MEMORY DHV

This five-minute, high-octane routine enables you to demonstrate that you possess a photographic memory. Later, you can also teach this routine to the girl. The act of teaching it is a good fifteen-minute routine in and of itself.

In order to perform this routine, you must learn a memory aid, known as a mnemonic device. A simple system, called the Peg System, works amazingly well.

First, memorize this rhyme: "One-Bun, Two-Shoe, Three-Tree, Four-Door, Five-Hive, Six-Sticks, Seven-Heaven, Eight-Gate, Nine-Line, Ten-Hen."

Once you've memorized this, you're ready to perform the routine.

The Effect

Pull out your trusty notepad and pen and write the numbers 1 through 10 on the paper. Tell your new friends in a set, "I need to pick your brain for four-point-two seconds. I need a list of ten random words. They don't have to be hard; they just have to be different." Write down a word next to each number.

Let's say for example she chooses the words (1) "dog," (2) "car," (3) "water," (4) "dancing," (5) "marijuana," (6) "outer space," (7) "ugly," (8) "airplane," (9) "straitjacket," and (10) "CD." After writing them down, without another glance at the list claim to possess a photographic memory. Then recite them forward, backward, and in random order. If she calls out a number, instantly answer with the word associated with that number. She'll think you're a genius.

The Secret

Memorize the words simply by *hanging them on the ten pegs in your memory.* Here's how. Word 1 is "dog." The first peg is "bun." Form a strange picture in your mind of a furry dog on a hot-dog bun—only with a live dog. This is a weird picture that you won't easily forget. In fact, the more absurd and emotionally evocative the visual association, the more memorable it becomes. Later, when she calls out the number 1, it's easy to make the connection in your mind: one = bun = hot-dog bun with furry dog = the word is "dog"! Do this with all the words on the list, and you'll be amazed at how vividly your mind stores and recalls information.

Another example: Let's say the fourth word she chose was "dancing." The fourth peg is "door." So picture a ballroom full of dancing doors. Later when you are trying to remember the fourth word she chose, you'll remember four = door = dancing doors = the word is "dancing"!

This same gambit can actually accommodate ten, twenty, even thirty more words. For example, let's say she chooses ten more words, for a total of twenty.

THE PEGS (SECRET)
One-Bun
Two-Shoe
Three-Tree
Four-Door
Five-Hive
Six-Sticks
Seven-Heaven
Eight-Gate
Nine-Line
Ten-Hen

CHOSEN WORDS
1. Dog
2. Car
3. Water
4. Dancing
5. Marijuana
6. Outer space
7. Ugly
8. Airplane
9. Straitjacket
10. CD

ADDITIONAL WORDS

11. Wind
12. Sailboat
13. Computer
14. Casino
15. Guitar
16. Books
17. Horny
18. Camera
19. Jogging
20. Paper clip

For number 1, you pictured a furry dog on a hot-dog bun. For 11, picture the same visual association for 1, only now imagine the dog is being blown around mercilessly in the wind. The image is a furry dog on a bun, then the dog in the bun getting blown over in the wind. Now you can remember that word 1 is "dog," and word 11 is "wind."

For word 4, picture a ballroom full of dancing doors. For 14, picture the same thing, except add many casino tables for games such as blackjack and roulette. Make sure the doors bump the blackjack tables after they dance. When stacking words and images across laterally, rely on your brain's natural tendency to remember sequences of action.

In this manner, you can continue to add additional lists, in groups of ten. Simply memorizing the Peg System rhyming scheme once and then practicing the routine several dozen times on random sets prepares you to perform this routine on-the-fly with any new set of randomly chosen words.

Part two of this routine is to teach it to the girl. Teach it on day 2 rather than the night you meet her. She'll need a quiet environment, no alcohol, and no interruptions for fifteen minutes to learn it from you. I enjoy demonstrating it as an opener (if I'm merging my current set with an adjacent set), using it in A2 to DHV to the group or as a reason to isolate the target. The lock-in prop I hand her right before the isolation? The notepad.

GROUP DYNAMICS:
LEAD THE MEN AND THE WOMEN FOLLOW.

There is safety in numbers, and women of beauty rarely go out alone. If I were to approach only women who were alone, I would drastically limit my options.

Single Set: **Is the target alone?**

Approaching singles, where the target is alone, appears deceptively simple compared to approaching groups. But without a group for which to DHV, you're left having to DHV directly to the target. Performed without skill, those DHVs can easily come off as bragging to her. What's more, the single can quickly turn into another set type if her friends arrive. In fact, be prepared for all set types to change abruptly (such as a single turning into a two-set, or a two-set turning into a three-set) at any time. But be especially on guard for this with singles. This phenomenon is known as an **external interrupt,** and you must be dynamic enough to alter your approach when this happens.

A single scenario has no *obstacles.* There she is. Approach her straight out. Don't wait for eye contact—too needy. Just approach her, and when she looks up at you, look her in the eye and smile. Always smile on the approach. It's less threatening.

If you see the girl from a distance and you've assessed the scenario as a single, you can wait there for her to notice you and then *immediately* go over. Or you can just go over without waiting. Caution: Do not establish eye contact and then fail to approach—and then think you can use that eye contact later to approach her. If you do this, you have *stalled out the set.*

By breaking the Three-Second Rule, you risk her thinking you wanted to approach yet chickened out. It's still *possible* to win the set, but you're now in damage-control mode.

Minimize the time between when the girl notices you and when you initiate the chat. Smile and enter, using any opener you please. Though you are opening her directly, it's from a screening frame, not a begging frame. You are curious about her and interested to find out more. In a single, the opening statement can be more direct than in another type of set: "I wanted to find out if there was more to you than meets the eye." Then stack to another, less direct opener.

Two-Sets: Is the Target with Another Person?

Compared to sets of three, four, or more people, the two-set is a uniquely challenging scenario. Roughly a fourth of all targets found in-field will be in a two-set.

Mark the friend of your target as your **obstacle.** Only when the obstacle is disarmed will he or she turn into a **friend.**

Don't go straight for the target if she is not alone. If you do, you will alienate her less attractive friend or, worse, her boyfriend, who will then act as a disgruntled guardian of the target and pull her away (or, in the case of the boyfriend, aggressively protect his investment from you, perceiving you as an invader).

You must win the *obstacle* over first. In fact, you can use this opportunity to *not* make eye contact with the target and actively ignore her. If she doesn't specifically feel ignored and overlooked, she won't feel the desire to engage you. When the target begins to talk, you may immediately neg her: "Why in the world would you interrupt your friend like that? Where were we? Oh yeah . . ." and then go back to your chat with the obstacle. The obstacle will laugh at your lighthearted, noninsulting negs. It will also make your high-value target feel briefly self-conscious. Use a lock-in prop on the target as you continue to talk to the obstacle, allowing the target to listen and receive your DHV spikes. Having been negged, the target will soon attempt to repair her image with you. She will then be chasing *you.* Continue to pepper negs into your DHVs. Finally, take the time out to pay her some attention in A3.

You cannot isolate the target if she is in a two-set, because that would leave the obstacle alone, which is seldom permitted. Nor would you want to isolate the target. As the preceding example demonstrates, the obstacle actually can be turned to your advantage.

But don't spend too much time conversing solely with the obstacle. Five to eight minutes is usually enough time to disarm and befriend him or her. Spending too much time may make the target believe the obstacle really likes you, prompting her to leave. Once you see that the obstacle likes you, clearly switch your attention over to the target. "[Target] and I like each other. Are you OK with that? As long as she doesn't speak, we're *gold,* Jerry! *Gold!"* Notice the obstacle-disarming shotgun neg.

Finally, in A3, you will show the target a sign that you like something about her by complimenting her—on her personality, not her anatomy. An example: "I can tell you are a leader of your friends. I like that."

It can be difficult to get a girl into isolation for comfort building when she is in a two-set. The reason is that she will feel bad at the thought of leaving her friend alone. It may be useful to have your **wing** come into your set, but only after you have reached the social hook point. He may then occupy the obstacle for you. In this way, you and your wing split the set, one girl for each.

If the obstacle is a boy, you're in what's called a mixed two-set. If a girl is with a boy, assume they are just friends and approach the group, initiating the chat with him. Befriend him. Once you've disarmed him, you've reached the waypoint where you ask, "How do you know each other?" He will tell you. If he's the boyfriend, you just made a new bud and didn't even introduce yourself to the girl, so you can't get in trouble. If he's not the boyfriend, she is now fair game.

Remember to neg her without insult in front of him. When she starts getting agitated or when she begins to try to get your attention, you can do a couple more negs and then finally pay attention to her. The guy will get out of the way and will watch you actually work the girl. You may be surprised how many times the guy just disappears altogether and is never heard from again.

Three-Sets and More:
Is the Target with Two or More People?

A two-set plus one wing equals a three-set. In three-sets, you may isolate the target. If you can't, just keep them together and work to build comfort with them. You can manufacture the opportunity to isolate her on another occasion.

A three-set is similar to the two-set, in that there is a target and an obstacle, but this one has an additional obstacle, and you must disarm both first. Again, you get the acceptance of these obstacles when you neg their friend (the target) and DHV. After you win the obstacles over and begin accepting the target's attention, you may ask the obstacles if it's all right to spend some time with the target for a moment. They will say yes because they like you. In fact, they may even spontaneously leave you two alone. In a two-set, the target may be reluctant to isolate with you in A3 because she doesn't want to leave her friend all alone. But in a three-set, when you isolate the target her friends still have each other.

- "Let's see what adventure awaits us in that room." (Put her on your arm, promenade-style.)
- "Hey, guys, I'm going to borrow your friend for a sec, we'll be right there on the couch."
- "Hey, guys, I've been ignoring your friend. I need to make it up to her. We'll be right back."
- "Your friend and I like each other; are you cool with that?" ("Uh, I guess . . .")
- "Is it OK if I borrow your friend for a second?" ("Uh, I guess, if it's OK with her . . .")
- "I like your friend. Is it all right if I talk to her for a minute?"
- "We kinda like each other—is that OK with you?"
- "I would very much like to see your friend again—is that all right with you?"
- "Great, then we'll be right back."
- "Good then can you give us just a minute, because I've got to get going."

In mixed sets, disarm all the males and find out what the relationships are before you IOI to the target.

PAWNING

With women of particular quality, it's often necessary to demonstrate preselection when gaming them. Before you open a set with a 10, for instance, you may first open an adjacent set with a 7 or 8, attract her, and put her on your arm. She is now your good-natured **pawn.** With this demonstration of preselection firmly in place, open the set with the 10. It should open easily due to your high perceived value. Your approach is also much less threatening with another woman on your arm.

At some point when you are in A3 with the 10, where she is earning your affections, you will be able to "choose" her over the 7. The 7 may then return to her friends, unharmed in any way.

A pawn can be paraded around the field to build social proof. She can be used to open sets—which will blast open with ease. She can be used to create drama or jealousy in later stages of the set as well.

Pawns are often unwitting participants in your game, although sometimes they are willing and "in the know."

PIVOTS

A pivot is a female friend whom you bring into the field in order to build social proof, open sets, create jealousy, and distract obstacles. In return for her services, you show her a good time and help her to meet guys. A well-trained pivot can be more useful than a good wing. The use of pawns and pivots makes you appear social.

FORWARD AND BACKWARD MERGING

As you gain experience in the field, practice merging sets. Be that social guy who introduces people to others. There are two principal types of merging: **forward** and **backward.**

To **merge forward** means to open a new set and merge your existing set into it. Pawning is often an example of forward merging.

To **merge backward** means to reopen a previous set and merge your current set back into it. This can be particularly useful because if your target is in a two-set, you will have trouble isolating her because her friend would be stuck alone. By merging them into another set, thereby creating a larger set, you can then isolate your target. ("We're going to sit right over there. Come join us in a couple minutes, but do give us a couple of minutes.")

Remember, you aren't just gaming the set but the entire room. Is anyone else merging sets in this room? Likely not. You must be the most sociable guy in here.

HOW TO PRACTICE YOUR GAME

+ **Do the MM Newbie Drill** for at least a month or two. Open three sets per hour, four hours per night, four nights per week.
+ Follow the Three-Second Rule.
+ Have an **opener** memorized, as well as a **neg** and a **false time constraint.** Also have one other routine ready to go before freestyling your set.
+ Practice your **delivery,** which includes body language, body rocking, voice tonality, a comfortable attitude, and a strong frame. Work on naturalizing your delivery through repetition.
+ **Release all expectation of outcome** and just enjoy the process like a new hobby.
+ Don't be picky about your sets—it's all just practice. Open mixed sets. There are a lot of good people to meet in this world.
+ Practice **locking in** to your set as early as possible.
+ Practice **multiple conversational threads** and **thread cutting.**
+ **Every other night, add a new routine** to your routine stack. Have at least one or two good stories to tell.
+ Have an **accomplishment intro** for your wing to throw into set. Have one for him, too.
+ Every few nights add a new neg, a false disqualifier, a roleplaying gambit, or some other canned material to your routine

stack. Practice them and get them up to speed. Eventually you'll need them to work without fail.

+ **If your mind goes blank,** have a standard procedure in place to handle the block. Prepare for it now so you don't have to deal with it later. Even experienced pickup artists go blank; they just have a few stories prepared for when it happens. For example, a specific routine is useful, as is giving a compliment and following it up with a question. Another strategy is to think of a question you might normally ask and rephrase it as a comment. Instead of asking, "How many brothers and sisters do you have?," say, "I bet you're the youngest in your family." Practice spontaneous conversation. It is better to get into a talkative state and talk about anything (simply be cautious not to DLV) than to say nothing. As long as you speak, you convey personality.

+ Push each set as far as you can just for the practice. Use **kino escalation** and **compliance testing** as much as possible. Kino escalation is by far the most important concept to master. (More on that in chapter 7.)

+ Feel free to go for phone numbers just for the practice. They won't amount to much—early on in your practice, these numbers will likely flake. Call them anyway just for the experience.

REVIEW

In the A2 phase, you **demonstrate higher value** to the set while simultaneously **negging** the target. She will respond with **indicators of interest,** which can be used to gauge your progress.

+ Some IOIs don't happen without a minimum amount of attraction. A girl may be attracted enough to sit down with you but not to leave the venue with you.

+ The most important IOIs are: She reinitiates conversation when you stop talking, she giggles, she touches you, and she tries to get rapport and build comfort with you.

+ **Passive IOIs** are sometimes the only IOIs she will give. That's why it's important to use **compliance tests** while gaming. Girls will occasionally give **fake IOIs** when it suits their purposes, although most of the time people are not consciously aware of the IOIs they are giving off.

+ There are also **indicators of disinterest, or IODs.** When a person gives an IOD, she conveys disinterest and an unwillingness to invest in the interaction.

+ A **neg** is an innocuous statement that only an uninterested party would say. Negs are actually a form of IOD.

+ There are three types of negs: the **shotgun neg,** which conveys lack of interest and disarms the group; the **tease neg,** which is cocky and playful and used for flirting; and the **sniper neg,** which causes the target to believe that she has done a DLV when in fact she has not. This creates embarrassment.

+ Anything you can do that conveys higher survival and replication value is a **demonstration of higher value,** or DHV.

+ Correspondingly, there is also a **DLV,** or **demonstration of lower value.**

+ Using a combination of DHVs and negs, the Venusian artist disarms and befriends the obstacles. This enables him to harness the social proof of the target's peer group. At the same time, the negs cause her to crave validation from him. She responds by giving IOIs. This is A2.

+ People who are well acquainted with one another tend to use **multiple conversational threads** while talking. New acquaintances tend to go from one complete thread to another in a more linear fashion. By using multiple conversational threads you can create the feeling that you and the target are already old friends. You also protect yourself from a conversational lockout.

+ When a certain thread is not useful to you, feel free to cut it and introduce a replacement. Sometimes this is necessary even when it is your own thread being cut.

+ "So, how do you all know each other?" is a question that usually arises in every set, and it tends to yield very useful information.

+ Stories should convey positive traits and personality and lead the listener through a fun series of interesting thoughts or emotional waypoints. The story doesn't have to be amazing or overly impressive, just engaging and enjoyable. Shorter is better.

+ Sometime during A2 you should be **locked in** to your set. You want to be leaning back against something while the girls face you, with their backs to the room.

+ While you are ignoring the target, lock her in using a **lock-in prop** to ensure she won't leave if she gets bored or distracted in the meantime.

+ A **pawn** is a girl who you have gamed and put on your arm solely to build social proof, to open sets, to create jealousy, and help her to meet guys.

7.

A3: MALE-TO-FEMALE INTEREST

She must be baited to invest herself in this interaction.

Once interest has been generated, the Game has only begun. In fact, it is a common mistake to think that attraction gets the girl. She must become **invested** in this interaction, and then rapport must be established. Attraction is useful—to bait her into investing. Other than that, attraction is but a vapor. She might be making out with you tonight, but that doesn't mean she'll return your calls tomorrow. We must now work to harness the initial attraction to get her to DHV us so we may IOI her.

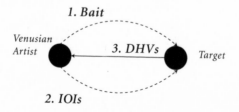

It could be said that *attraction is only a tool*. In A3, you will use her interest, combined with takeaways and screening, to bait the target into demonstrating value of her own. When she demonstrates value in an attempt to win you over, reward her with IOIs, then bait her again as the process repeats. In this way, her reward is tied to her investment. As she demonstrates value, she is simultaneously rewarded and baited to demonstrate more value.

This all comes back to pair bonding. A woman takes a much larger risk evolutionarily (and therefore emotionally) when she has sex. It's not enough that she is attracted to you—your pair bond must be there for her as well. She must have some assurance that when she is pregnant back in the cave you will stick around to bring her your fresh kills from the hunt. Otherwise you could impregnate her, move on to your next dalliance, and *she's screwed.*

Of course, we are speaking only of emotions. Is it really true that the pair bond "must" be there? Obviously not—one-night stands happen all the time. What is the meaning then?

The meaning is that the woman still has this emotional circuitry and it's still a factor in her behavior. Her emotions prefer a man of high value, high enough that it requires effort and investment in order to win him over. And her emotions *do* want to win him over. She wants to feel that he is pair-bonding to her.

In other words, she wants to feel that she is important to him not just as an attractive woman but as a specific woman. She needs to feel that it wasn't easy, that she had to invest and there was some fear of loss, but that now he is "falling" for her. His pair-bond circuits have curiously been turned on.

When you can bait a woman into working for your affections and you can convey your resulting "growing pair bond" effectively, you have mastered A3 and are ready to move into comfort.

FRAME CONTROL

The **frame** is the underlying meaning. It's the context, the implication—the unspoken assumption in everything you say.

If someone asks you, "Are the fish biting today?" then he is implying that you have been out fishing. He hasn't said so, but the listener will assume it is true—it's just part of the frame.

The frame supplies meaning to the content. For example, if some-one says, "Yeah, that guy got off," what is the meaning of that state-ment? Depending on the context, it could mean that the guy just got off of work, that he beat a rap at the courthouse and was set free, or that he had an orgasm—three completely different meanings. "Frame" determines which of those meanings becomes accepted. **He who controls the frame controls the communication itself.**

For this reason, when people interact with other people, they con-stantly play **frame games.** Through behavioral cues and subtleties in what they say, people convey their assumptions. If this conveyance is done with enough congruence, others will accept the frame as reality without thinking twice about it.

If your frame is strong enough, you can get away with anything. This concept underpins every piece of advice in this book. If you have the right frame and it is strong enough, you can break every rule and literally anything will work. Your approach might be wrong techni-cally, but she will still respond. For a newbie, buying drinks for girls is a bad move, but everyone has a story where someone bought drinks and still got the girl. Which is the right way? Buy her that drink or not?

The field will give you the answers that you seek. Go, and be in the field, and listen to your intuition there. Over time you will socially calibrate.

A woman will definitely test for congruence. If she can easily im-pose her frame over yours, it is a serious demonstration of lower value on your part. In fact, this DLV will most likely wreck any chances you had with her for sex. How can she rely on you to stand up to the big, bad world on her behalf, and on behalf of her offspring, if you can't even stand up to her? The security she feels from being with a strong man is a primary factor in her unconscious sexual selection strategy. What if you aren't naturally protective of your loved ones? Fake it 'til you make it. Practice makes perfect.

Beware: In the field, some men will also play frame games on you. If a guy can tool you in front of your set, he DHVs and can take your girl or girls. A woman will almost always choose the man with higher value and a stronger frame, and she will do it with little regard or loyalty to the fun little connection she had previously enjoyed with you. This may be true even if you are her boyfriend.

The only factor that counteracts this phenomenon is her level of investment in you—it will be psychologically much more difficult for her to jump to the next man if she has already invested a lot of time and effort in you.

HOOP THEORY

One frame game that people play is to see if they can get you to jump into their **hoops**. For example, a girl might try to get you to do something such as hold her purse or buy her a drink. Here are some additional examples:

- She gives you a fake IOI to see if you will start chasing her.
- She makes a comment to bait you into showing off to her.
- She gives a fake IOD to see if you get worried and react.
- She asks something to bait you into explaining yourself or apologizing to her.

These are all examples of hoops that girls will use to assert their feminine power. If you are doing things for a girl, chasing after her, showing off to her, reacting to her, apologizing to her, and explaining yourself to her, those are all IOIs that she can measure and exploit.

If you jump into her hoops, two things will happen. One, she will feel really good about herself—some part of her will be reassured on a primal level. And two, she may lose attraction. Just because she likes something doesn't mean that it will get you any closer to having sex with her.

Be careful. On one hand, you don't want to be the chump who gets tooled. On the other hand, you also don't want to be the social robot that is always playing power games when he should be relaxing and confidently enjoying his interactions with women. People aren't always trying to fuck with you.

When a hoop does come along, the average frustrated chump is *eager* to jump into her hoop. He thinks it shows her how much he cares.

He thinks it is romantic and will win her over. He thinks any guy who does otherwise is a *jerk*. But you don't have to jump into her hoop. You can turn it back on her. Or you can create a new hoop just for her. Or you can ignore it entirely—silence is often the best response.

Some examples:

PUT UP A NEW HOOP

Girl: *Why are you talking to me?*

You: *Do you always wear your lipstick like that?*

—OR—

You: [to her friends] *Is she always like this? Get this.* [start a routine]

IGNORE HER COMMENT

Girl: *What is with your shirt?*

You: (silence)

—OR—

You: *Hey, guys, get this. Last weekend, my friend and I* [start a routine]

GRAB HER HOOP

Girl: *Will you buy me a drink?*

You: *Buy me a drink and we will see*

Every conversation has some give-and-take. If she gives you a hoop, it is actually OK to jump into it, provided that you **first get her to jump into one of your own.**

Some examples of this:

EXAMPLE 1

Girl: How old are you?
You: Guess
Girl: Hmm . . . twenty-six?
You: Close. I'm actually twenty-eight.

In the first example, she asks your age. But instead of answering straightaway, you make her guess first.

In the second example, she tries the same trick back on you—but your frame is too strong!

EXAMPLE 2

You: How old are you?
Girl: Guess.
You: Do you want me to guess low or guess high?
Girl: Guess low!
You: Okay then . . . I'd say you you look about twenty-two.

An interesting thing about hoops is that **the more obvious it is that it's a hoop, the less likely someone will jump into it.**

For example, let's say someone asked you, "Hey, man, can you grab me a glass of water while you're up?" That's a pretty reasonable hoop, and most people would have no problem fulfilling such a request. What if instead he said, "Hey, goof. Why don't you get up, go in the kitchen, and get me some water like the little bitch that you are."

Indeed, few would jump into that hoop, which would be tantamount to accepting the frame that one is in fact his bitch. So . . . what you want to do is start small. Bait the target into innocuous little hoops: "Could you hold my drink for a sec? Thanks." Over time, as she falls into your frame, those hoops can become larger and more frequent. In the science of social dynamics, this process is known as **compliance momentum.** Soon she'll derive pleasure from rubbing your back and cooking your dinner, but for now start small by making her guess your age.

ROLE REVERSAL

In the previous chapter, I discussed how to create attraction through role-playing. A great role to play—probably the best one, in fact—involves having more social value than the target. In fact, this should be your reality, since she will otherwise find you less attractive.

Subtle cues in your behavior may betray your assumptions. So it's important that the frame you convey in those assumptions is one where she wants you and is chasing after you, whereas you are the one with higher value, you are the one who decides if you want to continue with her, and you are screening her to make sure she qualifies herself to you. If she is trying to embed DHV spikes into her stories, she is chasing you.

Notice that this strategy is exactly what a woman will use if you don't control the frame. Through little things that she says, she sets a frame that she is the prize. You don't want to get sucked into that frame. Instead, you want to grab this hoop and immediately use it yourself.

For example, a few minutes into the pickup, when you have some light kino (physical contact), you can say, "You know, you're really good at this." Without fail, she'll reply, "Good at what?" or "What exactly do you mean?" Your reply: "Your social skills just bought you three more minutes of my time. Good for you." Then smile and stack forward immediately.

Notice the unspoken assumptions: You are the prize, you are the one being chased, and you decide whether this will go to the next level (and the next phase). If you will take any girl you can get, you must be a loser. But if you are picky, you must be a winner, and her emotional circuitry is designed to respond to winners automatically. Attraction is not a choice.

Some examples of role-reversal lines:

- "Don't think you're going to get something just because you're buying me this drink."
- "Geez, are you always this forward?"
- "I don't want to rush things."
- "I don't want to get hurt. I need lots of comfort and trust first."
- "I want to get to know you better first."
- "I don't do that on a first date."
- "Hey, hands off the merchandise. This isn't free, you know."
- "I'll be the judge of that."
- "You just want me for my body."
- Take her hand, then as she reciprocates pull back and say, "Not so fast."
- "Are you always this fast?"
- ". . . yeah, if you're lucky."
- "I'm not ready to be in a relationship right now."
- "I wore my old briefs tonight to make sure nothing happens."
- "I swear, all you girls do is think about one thing."
- "Oh my God, are you groping me?"
- "You're a really nice girl." (This one is killer!)

+ "That guy over there looks perfect for you."
+ "I don't even know you."
+ "Let's just be friends."

The preceding lines are examples of what someone with the right attitude might say. Memorize some of them. Try them in your next set. See how things change in your favor. It's not the lines themselves that are important but the internal strength of frame that accompanies them. When you have strong **inner game,** the right things will come out of your mouth automatically. If your inner game is weak, learn gambits like the lines above to create the illusion that you are the prize. Soon you will be.

Also note that when you accuse her of being forward or of trying to get you into bed, that doesn't mean it's true. It's not—you are deliberately misinterpreting the situation. But if your frame is strong enough, she will get sucked in and respond as though it *were* true. Remember, she's programmed to respond to high-value guys.

HAVE STANDARDS

Here is what it means to have low standards regarding women:

+ I will take whatever I can get (which is not much).
+ There is nothing special or unique about you; I settled for you because I have no other choice for sex. I'm grateful just to find someone who is willing to fuck a loser like me; apparently that someone is you.
+ Being with me makes you feel common and used.

Instead, demonstrating to a woman that you have standards conveys this:

+ I have a lot of choice when it comes to women. I am accustomed to success with women.

✦ If I do take a liking to you, it is more than just for your looks. It is because you are a special and unique person who lives up to my high expectations.

✦ I will only be with a quality woman, and that's what you are.

Remember, women have antennae for this sort of thing. They can tell which way you lean, and they will feel the resulting emotions.

The average guy approaches a woman assuming that she is selective, and he hopes to pass her test. He thinks, *God, you are so hot. Do you have a boyfriend? Can I buy you a drink?* Because of this attitude, subtle cues in his behavior will convey entirely the wrong frame. Her hard-wired attraction circuitry will pick up on this, and she will lose interest.

Correspondingly, the opposite is true if you **have standards:** Subtle cues in your behavior will set the frame that you are a selective, high-value guy. She will pick up on this and gain interest. She expects that a guy with potential will be selective. Here are some standards worth considering:

✦ An attractive woman who takes care of herself
✦ A woman who is sociable and has friends
✦ A woman who has a real thirst for life
✦ A woman who has a great energy and a positive outlook
✦ A woman who is not a flake
✦ A woman who is in touch with her own sensuality; she's not a baby anymore
✦ A woman who can seek after her own fulfillment instead of waiting for approval from her friends
✦ A classy and smart woman with an education
✦ A woman who is adventurous and has a great imagination

SCREENING

The idea is to get *her* hoping that *she's* good enough to qualify for *you*. After all, you are a high-value guy. Sure, you're curious about her, but you want to know more. Is she smart? Does she have a lot of friends? Does she have a good relationship with her family? Can she dance well? (You know what *that* means!) What's the most spontaneous thing she's done recently? Can she cook?

- "Is there more to you than meets the eye?"
- "What do you want to be when you grow up?"
- "There are lots of beautiful women here. But what's really important is the energy, the intelligence, the little things about a person that make her unique. What are some things about you that would make me want to get to know you better?"
- "If a magician came along and you could be **poof** anything you want to be . . . what would you choose? And don't say princess."
- "Who are you?"
- "Do you like animals?"
- "How old are you?" (Now disqualify: "Oh my God, you're just a baby.")
- "So tell me, what are your three best qualities?"
- "Did you go to school? Are you smart? Do you have lots of friends?"
- "Can you cook? Do you give good backrubs? Are you adventurous?"
- "Are you a passionate person?"
- "There are some people who . . . they think they're open-minded and adventurous. They make all these great plans . . . they talk about meeting new people, or going on a diet, or taking a cool trip. But they don't. They just sit around doing the same old boring shit, over and over again. Are you like that?"

You don't want it to be explicit that you are screening her. Be very subtle, and she will realize it on her own accord, without thinking you're trying to make her feel screened. Somewhere in her mind an attraction switch will flip and she'll think, *Hey, this guy is screening me to see if he wants to invest more.*

She naturally assumes that the man she is looking for will be selective. It's a behavior that she's been expecting and thus is a powerful DHV. It sets the right frame, it's the signal she's been waiting for, and it baits her to invest.

So how can you convey to her in a memorized routine that she is being screened? Ask screening questions, give IOIs and IODs at the right moments, and convey real standards about the kind of people with whom you spend your time. It has to be true for you in order for her to feel congruence. You must also have some specific stories prepared allowing you to convey that you have standards.

INTERMITTENCE

Animal trainers know that it's much more effective to reward intermittently than consistently. Likewise, IOIs given to the target as a reward should not be delivered predictably. Uncertainty must be introduced to the equation to make the experience more compelling, so that she can feel a broader range of emotions such as hope, doubt, surprise, longing, fear of loss, and other forms of drama.

So the idea that we reward her with IOIs is only the simplest interpretation. In truth, we reward her investment with an intermittent and unpredictable mix of IOIs and IODs. This hot-and-cold, push-pull dynamic is very emotionally stimulating. When she is being rewarded in this manner, she is more likely to chase you and to comply with **compliance tests.**

....
Questions to Spark Investment

+ "What's your favorite color?"
+ "What did you think of high school?"
+ "What did you eat for dinner last night?"
+ "Have you ever been to the hospital emergency room?"
+ "How old where you when you first got drunk?"
+ "Did you and your siblings keep secrets?"
+ "Ever had a very rough breakup?"
+ "What's your favorite food, vacation, or place to visit?"
....

KINO ESCALATION

"Kino" is an abbreviation for "kinesthetic," which refers to the sense of touch. When Venusian artists speak of **kino,** they are referring to physical touching of any kind.

An important principle in the Game is that **nothing is ever a big deal.** The typical chump takes a girl out on a date and then hopes to get the kiss at the end of the night. He wants to show her how *respectful* he is. As the evening passes, he comes closer and closer to that awkward moment at the end of the night when he has to **make the big move** and go in for the kiss. This makes it a **big deal.**

If the moment of your first kiss is weird and awkward, it will probably also be your last kiss. Women are very unforgiving about this sort of thing. They have a fantasy about meeting the right guy, about how perfect it will be, about how everything will happen so naturally, and about how it will feel **so right.** And the truth is, with guys who have game (read: practice), that's exactly how it *does* happen.

When things go down the right way, there never is a "big moment" when you go in for the kiss and "make it happen." **Instead, there is a natural flow of kino from the very early stages of the set that leads all the way to the sex.** It should be seamless: a series of small, naturally executed moments, few of which ever stick out in any remarkable way. She feels like it's just a natural connection. Thus the kino begins in the early stages of the set and **escalates** from there.

Imagine two jellyfish floating near each other. A few of their tentacles just *barely* brush against one another at first. Tendrils curl and touch, sliding off and then touching again. More tentacles join the dance spontaneously. Larger numbers brush against one another as a few begin to pull more strongly. There is an energy between the two jellyfish, a powerful chemistry that builds as they intertwine and draw closer. You and your target are jellyfish.

There is no single moment when someone *makes a move.* Instead, it is this subtle, plausibly-accidental-yet-accelerating dance of about a dozen specific moves, some of them repeated so that there are often some thirty or more specific instances of escalation in a typical surge from the approach to mutual sexual fulfillment.

The innuendo, the little hints and touches, at first serve to add playfulness while creating plausible deniability. Do the touches induce the vibe or the other way around? It is all part of a snowballing or self-propelling system that feeds upon itself and sparks like a fire that grows until it becomes more than evident that **it is on** between you and your new female friend.

It is the specific pacing of escalating kino that is important, not the physical touches. The latter are not merely yards to be gained on a football field to move closer to the goal line. Rather, they are each a gambit to incorporate with various other tools and gambits for creating a certain *chemistry* between you and the target. There should be anticipation and tension in the air.

Windows of Escalation

As you game a girl—as you demonstrate value and lack of neediness, stimulate emotions, take control of the frame, make a connection, and so on—periodically a window of opportunity will open for you to escalate. If you miss the hint and that window closes, you have just demonstrated lower value. Soon her patience will wear thin. Miss enough open opportunities and she'll decide that you're either too chicken to make a move or incompetent in carrying it out. You don't want to appear as if you lack social intelligence and are thus incapable of leading the dance. Any of these are DLVs.

If she is standing there talking to you, just continue escalating. Always assume that it's on. This is also the best way to improve your calibration. Once your dynamic calibration is accurate, all of your escalations will happen smoothly, which is the long-term goal in building your skill set.

Some forms of kino include:

+ Arm in arm
+ Hands touching
+ Embracing
+ Embracing from behind
+ Kissing lips
+ Kissing or nibbling on neck

- Hand on knee
- Sitting on lap
- Arm around waist
- Touching face
- Smelling or pulling hair
- Hand on ass

Nonstandard Touching

When touching a girl's hand, you're *not* trying to set a frame that the two of you are explicitly "hand-holding" like a couple of teenagers marking their territory. Instead, you might be reading her palm, or thumb-wrestling with her, or showing her some jive handshake, or taking her hand and spinning her around in a playful little dance.

What's important is that as she becomes accustomed to your hands touching, this simple act should seem natural and normal to her. It shouldn't seem like you're trying to *get somewhere* with her, like it usually does when some guy wants to hold her hand or put his arms around her. Instead, it's fun and feels right as you create this comfort with your touch. Just don't let each touch persist until it becomes uncomfortable for her.

Don't Make Excuses

Don't be tentative and wimpy about touching—be natural and confident. Touching (guys *and* girls) is one way that alpha males like you demonstrate their dominance.

Always Lead—One Step at a Time

Remember the principle that it is easier to condition people to jump into small, innocuous hoops. Without realizing it, they fall into your frame as your hoops become larger and more explicit over time.

For this reason, when you do the spin maneuver, you don't say, "OK, I'm going to spin you around in a circle; let me see your hand." This is much too large of a hoop. Unless you have demonstrated a lot of value, girls will probably give you some trouble on this hoop; it forces their egos to become involved. Instead, say, "Go like this," as you hold out your hand, and then take hers when she mimics you. Then say, "Now do a little spin," as you spin her around. See how each step is easy for her to follow, bit by bit?

Lead her through the *entire* interaction in this way.

One Step Forward, Two Steps Back

While escalating, take one step forward, metaphorically speaking. At any sign of hesitation or defiance, take two steps back. Then step forward once again. For example, if you take her hand and you sense any hesitation, throw her hand away. Later when you take it again, she will comply more readily. The principle is that the "two steps back" creates **more discomfort** than the "one step forward." Thus the target becomes more likely to comply with future forward steps.

You Create the Tension, and You Push It Away

"Baby, we've got to slow this down. . . ." Some people think that it's the man's job to escalate and the woman's job is to resist. Instead, think of it as the man's job to do *both*. If you are constantly trying to get more kino, like gaining yards on a football field, it telegraphs far too much interest and deprives her of the hot-cold, push-pull energy that women find so compelling.

When you pull in close to a girl, tension hangs in the air. At some point, if she feels too much discomfort, she will pull away. This isn't what you want—you don't want to condition her into the behavior of pulling away from you. Rather, you want her conditioned to chase you.

So, once that tension has been created, it's now time to push *her* away. This might mean physically ("Get off me, jeez") or emotionally, such as using a back-turn, false disqualifier, or some other IOD. You might frame it as though you are the prize and *you're not going to let her get anywhere with you tonight 'cause you have to work tomorrow.*

When you push her away it spikes attraction. She will respond more playfully to you now. It also creates comfort. She doesn't feel like you're trying to *get something* if you're constantly pushing her away. This allows her to *feel safe* while having fun with you. She can allow the emotional stimulation to escalate instead of having to shut it off in self-defense. And the push makes it that much more stimulating for her when you do pull her back in.

For this reason, toss her hand away after thumb-wrestling or palm-reading. Devise a kino routine where you embrace her for a few seconds of role-playing, then push her away. Mix signals . . . draw near to her saying that it would never work out between you, but stroke your finger down her cheek at the same time. Then turn away. Use body rocking in conjunction with IOIs, IODs, false disqualifiers, role-playing, stories, and so on.

Kino Pinging

Kino pinging is an expression of growing attraction between two people. For example, if you push a girl's shoulder and she pushes yours back, the two of you are kino pinging. Soon people will be telling the two of you to go find a room. It's an indicator as well as a generator of attraction. Usually this sort of thing starts with a little verbal jousting back and forth. It's very easy to ping a girl and see if she will ping back. Kino pinging is similar to IOI pinging.

Sometimes kino pinging is more fun when it's deliberately hidden from her group. This shows discretion, builds conspiracy, and adds excitement.

TAKEAWAYS

Practice timing your back-turns and other IODs to coincide with sparks of attraction. Just at the moment when she feels most emotionally stimulated or in need of validation, turn away slightly, causing her to lean in a little more: "Wait, what were you saying about that little dog?" It takes practice to get the timing down. Remember, the attraction is only a tool to be used as bait.

When she pulls you back, intermittently reward her with IOIs. Isn't it interesting that a takeaway is best done just after a DHV, when the target has just experienced a spike in attraction? That is the time that she is most likely to chase to get you back. Similarly, it's best to give an IOD just before escalating, since it makes it more likely that she will accept the escalation. For example, if you turn your back on her just before you kiss her, she will be more likely to accept the kiss. These sorts of things must be experimented with in the field in order to be properly calibrated. Incidentally, this takeaway aspect of A3 corresponds to the third law of *The Tao of Steve: Be gone.*

This is a useful time to use sniper negs such as "eye boogers," "you spit on me," and "here's a napkin." Remember, you don't get blamed for the eye booger—God does. You aren't *trying* to make her feel embarrassed—it *just happened.* It is at this time that she wants to regain your respect and she wants to feel good again, so when you make your move she won't get all cocky and pull away. She'll accept it because she felt embarrassed and became quiet. Of course, don't reward her for being a goof, because that would be incongruent. So amp up her embarrassment by acting uninterested for a bit, then play nice guy and say, "Don't be embarrassed for being human." Then stop being "into" the conversation for a bit. In that state of mind, she is extremely susceptible to escalation.

COMPLIANCE

One concept central to the Mystery Method is **compliance testing.** Request your target do something for you, be it hold your drink, hold your arm, scratch your back, kiss you, or spread her legs.

If she complies with your move, several things are accomplished: First, similar to kino pinging, it is an IOI ping and also creates attraction. Second, you have escalated—she is now more comfortable with your touch. Third, her frame has been further influenced and absorbed by your own. Reward her with an IOI, but do so intermittently. You might do a compliance test with her hands and then throw them away. But then her next compliance might be rewarded with a compliment or another touch or by turning to face her more with a smile, etc. This might be followed by another IOD to create more sexual tension.

COMPLIANCE TEST IOIs

- ✦ You take her hand and drop it . . . she grabs for it again
- ✦ You squeeze her hand and she squeezes back
- ✦ You touch her and she touches you back
- ✦ You put her hand on your knee and she leaves it there
- ✦ You put her arm in yours and walk her around the venue. She complies
- ✦ You sit her on your lap. She allows it
- ✦ When you are locked in, you take her hand and pull her in a little closer as you are talking at the same time. Now she is standing between your legs as you run game on her.

THE KINO TEST ROUTINE

Hold out your hands in front of you, with your palms facing up. The body language to her should communicate that you are expecting her to give you her hands. This is a compliance test.

If she gives you her hands, squeeze them, and see if she squeezes back. Then slowly lower them, and see if she follows the movement in order to continue contact.

- ✦ Try throwing her hands away after.
- ✦ Try telling her she passed or failed.
- ✦ Try explaining the routine as you perform it on her.
- ✦ Try it as merely subtext while talking about something else.
- ✦ Try using this routine on the target as a way of defeating a competing male who has invaded your set.

If she defies your compliance test, give her an IOD, followed by a DHV and then another compliance test. For example, if you ask a girl to stand up, she may not. She has refused your hoop. This doesn't look good; it's a DLV to the group.

Don't blame her—maybe she's just not attracted enough yet, or maybe the hoop was too big, too early. So just be unaffected, do another DHV, and try another, smaller compliance test: "Show me your hand" (which can always be followed up by taking her hand and saying, "OK, now stand up for a sec. . . .")

There are hundreds of compliance tests. Tell a girl to sit closer. Kiss a girl. Ask her any question. Hold her hand. Rub her neck. Put her hand on your cock. Every escalation, every bounce or move, every touch, even sex itself is a compliance test. When you're wondering how things are going with your current target, ask yourself: Where is her compliance threshold level at now?

If you are ready to raise the bar on her threshold level, DHV and compliance-test again. The more value you have, the more she'll permit you to escalate your compliance testing. If you're the "Misunderstood Superstar," her resistance to escalation goes right out the window.

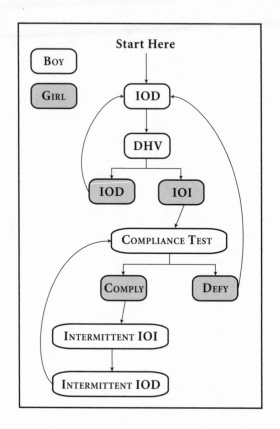

Compliance Momentum

There is a basic MM model where people interact socially in five ways:

1. **DHV**—Demonstration of Higher Value
2. **DLV**—Demonstration of Lower Value (other people do this, not you)
3. **IOI**—Indicator of Interest
4. **IOD**—Indicator of Disinterest
5. **CT**—Compliance Test (almost all interactions at some point come down to a test for compliance; will you get compliance or defiance?)

Here is the way it goes after you open: You IOD (neg, etc.) and DHV, then look for female IOIs. If she responds with IOIs, give her a compliance test. (If instead she gives an IOD, then just repeat the process.) If she complies with your test, reward her with IOIs and then give her another compliance test. As this cycle repeats, **compliance momentum** is built.

This continues until you reach sex, which occurs somewhere around 65 percent compliance. (Yes, there are deeper levels of compliance than sex—but they are not the subject of this book.)

Comfort is not only trust and time; it is also compliance. If you ask a friend to do something for you, he is much more likely to do it than if you were to ask a random stranger. If you walk up to your girlfriend and kiss her, she will not only let you; she will pull you in and kiss you harder. Why? Because you have a high level of compliance. However, you have almost no chance of walking up to a stranger and doing the same things and receiving the same responses.

Why do we say that compliance has momentum? All compliance builds upon itself. Someone complying will continue to comply. Someone defying will continue to defy and resent, and interpret any attempt to force her to comply as an attack. But once we have reached compliance threshold, it takes very little effort to keep the compliance going.

Negative Compliance

Tens will not usually want to talk to you right off the bat. They will exhibit low compliance to your opener. So to establish compliance, IOD them, DHV, then try to see if they will comply.

This may not be necessary if you already have compliance. For example, what happens when you open a set of 7s and immediately the girls are into you—only you neg them purely out of dogmatism? In an instant, the interaction goes sour.

Why? It's because you have established **negative compliance.** You punished them for good behavior. The same phenomenon occurs when you reward bad behavior (or fail to punish it). Either way, negative compliance gets built up and then works to your detriment.

Compliance Threshold

When choosing to align with people, we comply with their requests *to a certain threshold.* The more value that you represent to a woman, the more she wants to align with you. Hence, the more leeway you have when escalating. By using IODs to punish defiance and IOIs to reward compliance, a Venusian artist can quickly bring a woman to her compliance threshold.

The **compliance threshold** is the point of the interaction where she realizes that she has more fun if she complies! Once this happens, you have established control of the frame and she will follow your lead. This should happen in A3. *If you are still getting defiance in C1, then you're not really in C1 after all.*

Don't be afraid to overestimate your value. If you waste time trying to build value that you already have when you should instead be compliance-testing, you could blow yourself out of the set by creating negative compliance.

One Venusian artist used to have a problem with Southern girls because they were *so* nice that he felt he wasn't sparking attraction. Therefore he would overneg to the point of becoming obnoxious. Later he realized that those sets were already on and all he was doing was creating resistance to his compliance tests by punishing inappropriately, when in fact he should have been escalating.

Give-and-Take

Mutual compliance occurs in C1. In A2, if she drops something, you bust on her for it. You do not give her any of your compliance yet. However, in the comfort stage, if she drops something, pick it up for her. It's here that you show that you will comply for her. This is attractive, as she wants someone to take care of her. She just doesn't want it until mid-game.

Once in comfort, the Venusian artist and his target should both comply for each other all the way to a mutual seduction. Having a girl undress you is better than you undressing her. If you get a girl to come over and bring a candle and then light it for you in your bedroom, things are going to happen—the compliance makes it clear.

It's also important to note that her willingness to comply will be directly affected by the congruence with which you deliver the compliance test. If you give her a compliance request and any part of her senses you cannot back it up, she will deny you. Do not look for her approval or even her being "OK with it." Just lead.

What are some other examples of gaining compliance?

+ Getting her to invest. (She goes to retrieve a drink for you; she spends some money on you, etc.)
+ Getting her to move with you or bounce to another location.
+ Locking her in: The longer a girl wears an item of yours, the more compliance you have. If the girl removes your item, she is defying.
+ Social pressure: Get one of her peer group to tell her to be nice to you or to give you an accomplishment introduction and you will immediately gain much more compliance from her.

People generally comply if it results in more fun, or gaining some benefit. We are inherently selfish. People will also comply if there is a threat. A man with a gun gets more compliance than one with a hose.

Of course, the Venusian artist will never actually pull out a gun. But there are other ways to punish defiance. For example: You can punish her with freeze-outs every time she defies. Any IOD will work. When freezing her out, it's much better to seem like you are becoming **genuinely distracted**—you do *not* want her to think that you're deliberately punishing her. (See chapter 8 for more on this.)

You can walk off in the middle of her defiance and start a jealousy plotline in an adjacent set, then either wait for her to come over or just wander back after establishing how much fun you can be. (See chapter 8 for more on freeze-outs and jealousy plots.)

In early A2, you can take all attention off of her and use active disinterest, then compliance-test again and IOI her for complying.

Token Resistance

At higher levels of escalation, such as kissing, your hands will be moving much more freely around her body. (This is also a form of compliance testing.) Girls are culturally programmed to give **token resistance** to physical escalation; it's a response to avoid feeling like a slut. She wants things to happen, but she wants it to feel right and she doesn't want it to be *her fault*. For example, if you put your hand on her leg and leave it there, she may remove it. This is undesirable because you are now using her **anti-slut defense** to condition her to push you away.

But instead if you stroke your finger up her thigh as part of a routine and then your touch is gone, you have ended clean. She may even feel slight disappointment that the touch is gone. Now she is being conditioned to feel dismay when your touch is gone.

She is also more accustomed to your touch and accepting of it. This works because of the **consistency principle**. She didn't object because the touch was already gone. But by not objecting some part of her has tacitly accepted that it's not objectionable. In the future, she is more likely to be consistent with the behavior and frame that she is already accustomed to when interacting with you. After all, she's not a hypocrite.

Touching with Motion

Another interesting aspect of that example is the **motion** involved. Somehow moving your hand across her thigh is not as objectionable as putting your hand on her thigh and leaving it there.

Similarly, if you are ready to touch her breasts outside her shirt, you will gain compliance much more easily if instead of just grabbing her boob, you stroke your hand across it as part of a larger petting motion on her body, with your hand ending up somewhere else, like her waist. It's just a way of escalating more smoothly, which she will appreciate. Make her feel good.

Qualifiers

Periodically, the time comes to let a girl know she is qualifying for you. She has to feel like she is winning you over; otherwise, she will get discouraged.

These lines are only examples. You could qualify her even with your body language. Try giving her an IOI. Turn to face her when she says something that you can misinterpret as being cool and worthy of an IOI. Often, it's useful to follow an IOI with an IOD. Notice that each of these qualifiers has an optional disqualifier:

- "You are *so* adorable . . . it's sickening."
- "You know, you can be pretty interesting sometimes."
- "You're awesome! Just kidding."
- "It's weird . . . I feel so good around you." (False disqualifier) "Too bad you're not my type."
- "You're pretty . . . and *evil*."
- Oh my God, you're a dancer? That is so awesome. I can't even talk to you now."

Statement of Interest (SOI)

An indicator of interest is usually a subtle cue of some sort, whereas a **statement of interest** (SOI) is an explicit verbal statement making clear your growing interest in her. For example, buy her a drink and say one of the following:

- "When we met, you just seemed like another one of those California blondes, but since I've gotten to know you, I actually feel nervous around you now."
- "Oh my God, I can't believe this. Can you believe we met at a bar?"
- "We're going to sit down over there; would you like to join us?"
- "You know what? You are actually pretty cool. I'm curious about you."
- "I have to hang out with you again sometime. Can you cook?"

A well-timed SOI can work wonders.

Compliments

- No crap about "you are so hot," "you are my dream girl," etc. In other words, compliment from a screening frame, not a begging frame.
- Compliment her style, her energy, her poise, or something unique about her outfit that she chose. Don't be that guy who is constantly complimenting girls on their necklaces. Learn to **notice things.**
- Try giving her a compliment followed by a screening question.
- Try using constructive criticism after making the compliment. This is a powerful way to neg her and demonstrate value.
- **DON'T MENTION HER LOOKS.**

Try complimenting her in a way that directs her to behave the way you want her to and to play a role that's useful to you. Here's an example:

"You seem to be very connected with your emotions. You seem to really listen to your woman's intuition." Or if she's being rude (or if you want to misinterpret that she was rude), say, "You're too classy to act like this."

Just tell her how you "view" her and she will become that person for you—but only if she agrees and it is flattering for her. You are building a character for her, and she will play the role because she likes the way that the role makes her feel. Here are some *examples* of compliments:

- "You seem like someone who really knows what she wants. I admire that."
- "You really care about your friends. I bet you will make a really good mother."
- "You have a good energy."
- "I notice you're the leader of your friends. Why is that?"
- "You're a great conversationalist."
- "You're a very classy girl. What are you doing in a place like this?"
- "Wow, you seem so confident with your friends, like you're kinda the leader of your peer group. I just love your energy. . . . Are you close with your family?" (Going into next routine.)
- "You have such an expressive personality . . . That's a valuable thing in the entertainment industry. There are a million women who are beautiful; I was just in California, but how many do you think have an outgoing personality like yourself? I'm telling you, that's a very attractive quality and a valuable asset."

Bait—Hook—Reel—Release

The **bait—hook—reel—release** fishing-for-investment metaphor is one that continually resurfaces in study of the Game. One way to apply it is in A3. You want to give IOIs to the target, but you don't want to seem too easy. (Otherwise she won't value your pair bond; instead, she will enjoy your IOIs as a validation of her sexual power, but she will lose attraction for you.)

The idea is to make the *woman* demonstrate higher value to *you*. **Bait** her into telling you *interesting things* about herself (not "What do you do?") so when she replies (**the hook**) you can IOI her (**reel her in**) only to push her off again (**release** her from the pressure of being hit on). This process repeats several times.

Here is an example for you to use in-field right away:

You: *[Bait] What nationality are you?*
Her: *[Hook] French.*
You: *[Reel] Seriously? No way! The girl I had the biggest crush on in high school was French! [Release] I can't even talk to you now.*

Every time she gives you a demonstration of higher value, indicate your interest to her. This way she will believe your IOIs, and when you fully SOI her, she will feel like she really deserves it. This allows your attraction for her to legitimately grow over several minutes, instead of just IOIing her because she first IOIed you.

An important aspect of the Mystery Method is to restructure routines to be in context with **your particular identity**. Take the time to write up some personalized routines with this in mind. Again, make yours congruent with your identity. You do not have to be a magician to do the Mystery Method, but you do need a strong identity.

Here is an example, using my identity:

Mystery: *If you could be anything in the world with no chance of failure, what would you want to be? And don't say princess.*
Girl: *Um, an actress.*
Mystery: *Really? When I was little I wanted to grow up and be a magician. And you know what I am now? A magician! So you want to be an actress. I'm living proof that our dreams can come true. It would be so cool if you were an actress. I love that! We need to figure out how to make that happen. I bet you'd be an amazing actress. But what if you get more attention than me? I can't even hang out with you now.*

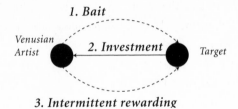

1. Bait

Venusian Artist ● ←— *2. Investment* —→ ● *Target*

3. Intermittent rewarding

The **bait—hook—reel—release** metaphor perfectly matches the A3 process described in this chapter, whether applied to screening, hoops, kino escalation, or compliance testing. Here are some examples:

Bait—challenge her
Hook—she DHVs for you
Reel—give her an SOI
Release—false disqualifier

Bait—give her a compliance test
Hook—FAILURE; she defies
Release—give her an IOD

Bait—DHV in some way
Hook—she gives IOIs
Reel—kino escalation
Release—throw her hand away

Bait—give her a compliance test
Hook—SUCCESS; she complies
Reel—kino escalation
Release—push her away

Bait—ask her a screening question
Hook—she qualifies herself to you
Reel—give her an IOI
Release—false time constraint

Bait—DHV, then takeaway
Hook—she chases; for example she quickly finds a way to prolong the conversation
Reel—give her a qualifier
Release—give her an IOD

Bait—give her a hoop to jump into
Hook—she jumps into your hoop
Reel—reward her for doing so
Release—shut up

Bait—give her a compliance test
Hook—she complies
Reel—compliment her
Release—tease neg

The bait can be a challenge, a screening, a screening question, a compliance test, a takeaway, a hoop, or so on. *These are only examples.* The truth is that bait can be *anything.* It can be a subtle cue in your body language. It can be an allusion to a tempting bounce, giving her an opportunity to show interest in joining you. Find what works for you through experimentation and field-testing.

You: *How old are you?*
Her: *Twenty-three, how about you? [Hook]*
You: *[Ignoring her question] Hold out your hand.*
Her: *[She complies—spin her.]*
You: *How graceful! I bet you were a ballet geek.*

You: *[Hold out hands, expecting hers.]*
Her: *[Complies and gives you her hands. Hook!]*
You: *[While talking about unrelated material, do the kino test.]*
Her: *[She squeezes back.]*
You: *[Continue talking and throw her hands away.]*

You: *What do you want to be when you grow up?*

Her: *I want to be a teacher . . . I'm studying education at [XYZ] School [Hook!]*

You: *Wow that's a good school. This is funny, I thought you were like these other girls; I gave you way insufficient credit. I bet you'd be really good working with children; you'll probably make a great mother someday. Too bad you're totally not my type. You're a cool girl; we should find you someone tonight.*

You: *[Finishing a DHV]*

Her: *So what's your name? [IOI]*

You: *[Ignoring her question] Are you an intuitive person?*

Her: *Yes, very much so! [Hook!]*

You: *Let me see your hand.*

Her: *[She complies.]*

You: *[Stroking your finger down her palm.] Interesting. . . . [Throw her hand away.]*

Her: *Wait, what? Can you read palms? [Chasing]*

You: *[Taking her hand again.] See this line? This is the retard line; it means you're a retard. [Hug her.]*

You: *So tell me, what are your three best qualities?*

Her: *Well, I'm loyal, I'm smart—[Hook!]*

You: *[Interrupting] Can you cook?*

Her: *Oh yeah. I can cook all kinds of stuff. [Hook!]*

You: *[Smiling approvingly] That's so cool. It seems like everyone eats TV dinners these days. I have to go in a minute, but I was wondering . . . [Go into next routine.]*

You: *[Finishing a DHV and body rocking away . . .]*

Her: *So wait a sec: what ever happened to that dog? [Hook!]*

You: *[Rocking back] You know what, you're so adorable . . . it's sickening!*

HER PERCEPTION OF THE PICKUP IN TERMS OF SOCIAL STATUS

When you first open her set, you are just some guy. She has no reason to perceive you as having any more value than that. She sees herself as the prize.

A1

Except...hmm, you are dressed well and have good body language, are not needy, and interesting...

A2

Now you are demonstrating value. Other girls are touching you and then you neg her! She starts to give IOIs, which you exploit.

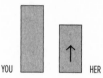

She DHVs to win your affections. You respond with intermittent IOIs, compliance tests, and hoops as she "wins you over."

A3

Now that she has indicated her interest in you (A2) and you have indicated your interest in her (A3), she is invested in this interaction and is probably trying to build comfort with you, or wishing you would make it happen.

C1

You now have mutual respect, investment, and attraction. Move her to a location where the two of you can be more isolated together, and build comfort with her. Don't forget to calibrate your kino to her comfort levels.

REVIEW

+ In the A3 phase, you bait a woman into working for your affections. As she becomes invested in the interaction, you reward her with indicators of interest, and the cycle repeats.

+ The **frame** is the context, usually assumed and unspoken, that provides meaning to the content and the interaction. He who controls the frame controls the communication itself.

+ **If your frame is strong enough, you can get away with anything.** You can use any opener, any line, any spontaneous attitude, and it will work—**but you must be congruent.**

+ **The field will give you the answers that you seek.** Go, and be in the field, and listen to your intuition there. Over time you will calibrate.

+ Women and men will play frame games on you and test you for congruence. Women are seeking a strong mate and men are competing for dominance. Often this is unconscious and instinctive behavior.

+ There are all sorts of hoops that people will produce to see if you will jump. Don't. Instead, bait them to jump into your hoops.

+ Don't go off the deep end and respond to every social interaction like it's a power play for dominance and like you are so clever for recognizing it. You will turn into a **social robot** and will lose your ability to vibe naturally with people. Be relaxed and enjoy the process.

+ Feel free to jump into someone's hoop if you can first make her jump into one of yours.

+ The more obvious it is that it's a hoop, the less likely it becomes that someone will jump into it.

+ A useful frame is where you are the person in the interaction with the most value. This isn't explicitly communicated, but you imply it with your assumptions, in a fun way.

- When using canned material, remember that what's really important is the **inner game.** With practice, your internal frame will become congruent and comfortable with spontaneous interaction as well as canned material.

- You must **have standards** about what sort of woman you want to be with. This will be communicated in your frame through many subtle cues in your body language and speech.

- One way to show your standards is to screen her by asking her certain questions. Calibrate gently—you don't want her to think this is a tactic to flip her attraction switch. (The standards must be real.)

- Intermittent rewarding is more effective than consistent rewarding. Use IODs to add a **hot-cold, push-pull** dynamic when you are stimulating and rewarding the target.

- There is a natural flow of kino from the very early stages of the set that leads all the way to sex. Nothing is ever a big deal; there is never any "big move." It's just how the two of you are when you are together.

- Takeaways, properly timed, will condition her to chase.

- Almost all interactions at some point come down to a test for **compliance.** Will you get compliance or defiance?

- **Compliance momentum** can be built by rewarding "good" behavior using intermittent IOIs and punishing "bad" behavior using IODs. A Venusian artist will continue compliance testing all the way up to sex.

- The **compliance threshold** is the point where she realizes that she benefits more if she complies.

- Don't compliment a woman on her looks. Don't even mention her looks.

- **Bait-hook-reel-release** is a metaphor used to describe the application of compliance testing, screening, qualifiers, and other aspects of A3.

8.

....

CONVERSATION

A wide conversational rapport
A sense of comfort and trust
A sense that this interaction is real and genuine
A feeling of connection

There are several elements that need to be added to the mix at this point. Although you and your target have both indicated interest in each other, you still have only known each other for five or ten minutes. Your interest is based purely on the attraction switches flipped. By baiting her to invest further, you now have an opportunity to build comfort and trust with her. And that is what actually gets the girl—**the Game is played in comfort.** Everything else was merely to get to this point.

If it has not already been demonstrated that the two of you can have a normal, fun, natural conversation together, this is the time to do so. In the future, when she is deciding whether to return your phone call, you don't want her thinking, *Jeez, all we really had to talk about was dog food and petting our dogs; we didn't really connect on a conversational level. Plus, I made out with him, so I know he's going to want more of that, but I don't even know this guy . . . it was fun at the time, but I just don't feel comfortable with this right now. There are a million guys; I'll meet another hot guy tonight when I'm out with my girlfriends.*

This reason is exactly why so many phone numbers are flakes—not enough comfort. Thus it's important to have fun, natural conversations with girls, using wide rapport and multiple conversational threads. When she looks back on that conversation, she should be thinking about how much she enjoyed talking with you and looks forward to doing so again.

Also, there must be a sense that this interaction is real and genuine. Often this is why women distrust "nice guys." How does she know he isn't just pretending to be nice in order to get into her pants? Sure, he's buying dinner and telling her she's pretty . . . but is that what he's really like? Or is that just what he's like when he wants something?

By demonstrating a willingness to walk or to step up and call bullshit in a fun way, you demonstrate that you are being genuine with her, which creates **trust,** allowing her to **feel safe.** This is what girls mean when they say they want a man who can **keep it real.** A girl needs to feel that she is getting to know the **real you**—and that takes time.

When you first game a girl, she is being stimulated and having fun with you. If this is done in a competent manner, most women enjoy it at the time. But for her to consider dating you in the future, she must not only be invested; she must feel a real connection between you. She must see you as someone who could really become a part of her life— and, more important, that she could become a part of *your* life. She wants someone who is similar to her in various ways. She wants someone who looks like a good counterpart, who will make other people say, "Oh, you look like such a great couple!" She wants someone her friends like; someone she can show off on social occasions; someone she understands and empathizes with; someone who has a social circle she could see herself joining.

When she remembers you, does she feel a genuine connection? Or are you just some guy she had a few laughs with while drinking at a bar one night?

THE FREEZE-OUT

When you are in the **attract phase,** you can bust her balls when she busts yours. But once you reach comfort, if she busts on you, you can only **freeze-out** by withdrawing attention. She will say, "What's wrong?" You say, "Nothing." *(Not sulking! The delivery must be sincere, like it's really no big deal.)* Then, after she is punished by your silence for an awkward moment, return to comfort by finding something to IOI her for.

She learns quickly not to bust on you because (1) you've already proven that you *can* bust back (in attract phase) and (2) she feels *discomfort* whenever she busts on you. This is your opportunity to show her you aren't always cocky-playful like you were in attract phase.

So *freeze-outs* are a way to *train* her. You can use discomfort sparingly to teach her that being nice to you means comfort and fun. When the time has come to build comfort, it's counterproductive to continue being cocky and ball busting. The punish-reward dynamic must be used instead.

This phase is also your opportunity to demonstrate your ability to make uncomfortable situations comfortable again. Here it's great to use **sniper negs,** like saying, "You have something on your nose," and then handing her a tissue. She feels uncomfortable, but it's not *your* fault. It's God's. Right after this, she will feel *so small.* After she notices that you are freezing her out a bit—not as if you're being cruel but rather as if you aren't interested in her—give her a **compliance test,** and then reward her compliance with an IOI. In this way you can continue rewarding her but only for compliance, not misbehavior.

COMFORT-BUILDING LOCATIONS

The location where you first encounter a woman is not necessarily favorable to building comfort. The music may be too loud for lengthy comfort-building dialogue. The space may be too congested. Your romantic interest's protective friends, current boyfriend, jealous ex-boyfriend, or family members may be present in some combination. You or she may also lack the immediate time to spend seven hours building enough comfort with each other.

If the meeting location does not allow you the time or afford a comfortable setting to sit with her and build comfort, you must move her from the meeting location to a comfort location. All comfort-building locations are quieter and more secluded (though often still public) settings where you, your romantic interest, and her friends (as well as your friends) may share in lengthy dialogue.

THREE COMFORT-BUILDING LOCATION TYPES

There are three types of comfort-building locations that you and your romantic interest will visit. The Mystery Method terms these C1, C2, and C3.

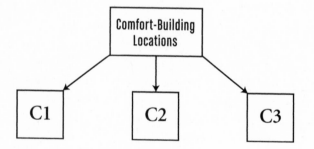

C1 = Any comfort-building location within the meeting location.

C2 = Any comfort-building location separate from the meeting location and the sex location.

C3 = Any comfort-building location within the sex location.

THE FIVE LOCATION TYPES FOR GAMING

The five locations are the meeting location, C1, C2, C3, and the sex location. The C1 location exists somewhere within the meeting location during the pickup stage, while the C3 location exists within the sex location during the seduction stage.

Here's one way to look at it:

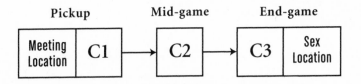

There are several reasons for this design structure:

+ Moving only a few feet from the meeting location to the C1 location carries with it much less of a safety risk for a woman who has just met you.
+ It is much less of a personal investment in getting to know you, a relative stranger, than jumping directly to a C2 location without establishing at least some comfort. **Because it's a smaller hoop, she's more likely to do it.**
+ Moving to a C1 location allows you the opportunity to make her feel comfortable enough that you may successfully jump to a C2 location with her.
+ Moving only a few feet from the C3 location to the sex location is much more practical than having her know in the C2 location that you are planning on taking her directly to a sex location with only one "naughty-thoughty" on your mind.

Going from the meeting location to a C1 location, or from the C3 location to the sex location, is called **moving.** Going from C1 to C2, from C2 to another C2, or from C2 to C3, is called **jumping.**

THE C1 LOCATION: ANY COMFORT-BUILDING LOCATION WITHIN THE MEETING LOCATION

Unless your romantic interest is already sitting in a quiet area within the meeting location, you will inevitably have to **move** from the meeting location to C1.

In fact, before you even approach a woman in a meeting location you must have a nearby C1 comfort-building location preselected and be prepared to move to it.

C1 examples:

- ✦ Leaning up against wall or bar with woman leaning in and facing you
- ✦ Sitting on stool by bar with woman standing between your legs
- ✦ Sitting in quiet area of club or coffee shop

Unless your meeting location is already a good C1 location, every successful pickup will inevitably require you to **move** to a C1 location.

MOVING TO C1

To **move** means to go from the meeting location to C1 with your romantic interest and her friends, if necessary. (Moving also means going from the C3 location to the sex location, which I'll examine in a later chapter.) Moving is not only a logistical necessity but also a powerful comfort builder in and of itself.

Example: I'm speaking to a beautiful woman by the bar of a busy

nightclub. Before even approaching the woman in this meeting location, I had my game plan already in mind: moving her to the quiet
smoking section, a good C1 location. I place my hat on her and say,
"I'm going to show you something really neat. Come join me for a
sec."

The woman replies, "Where are we going?"

"It's a special little place I like to call . . . you'll see." I laugh, pointing
toward the smoking section. "Just right there." I begin walking off a
few feet.

While she is hesitant to leave her friends even "for a sec," she is more
apt to join me because I have locked her in with my hat. Though she
doesn't even smoke, she has to at least take a few steps forward to return my hat.

"What are you gonna show me?" she asks curiously as I grab her
hand and lead her through the crowd.

"Are you creative?" I ask back, keeping her curious. While we move,
I do a subtle *interest test* on her, that is, gauge her interest level by loos-
ening my grip as we walk. Does she hold my hand tightly still or let go
of it?

"I want to see how creative you are before I show you," I say as I
pull out a pad of paper and pen and then hand them to her. Upon
reaching the smoking section, we sit together and I place her hand
on my knee and let go. Does she leave it there? This is another subtle
test.

I lean back and say, "It's quieter out here. OK, I need you to think up
a list of ten random words, but they can't have any association with
any other word you come up with."

And so, with a successful move (and an isolation from her friends
as well in this case) from the meeting location to C1, I am able
to begin building comfort, in this case by demonstrating my
photographic memory using the Peg System and then teaching it
to her.

CONVERSATIONAL RAPPORT

- Be a talkative person. Talk to anybody, not just girls. Get into the zone.
- Don't explicitly try to impress or show off. Don't directly tell impressive facts about yourself. Don't seek attention, approval, or understanding from others. Guys who are worried about what hot women think already bother them enough. Try being the one guy who isn't worried.
- Don't talk about weird, creepy, or stupid topics. Most people who do this are seeking attention. *It's cool to get attention, but it's very uncool to be perceived as seeking it.* Thus don't provoke people or show off to them in any way.
- Practice moving your target and getting her into isolation for comfort building.
- Demonstrate **vulnerability** and establish **commonality** and **connection.**
- Practice stacks of canned material. This is a useful skill.
- Practice natural, spontaneous conversations with no canned material.
- Practice using multiple conversational threads.
- Continually escalate kino and use compliance testing.
- Cut boring threads: yours or hers. Lead the frame.
- Talk about fun, interesting, emotionally compelling topics.
- Don't ask a bunch of questions. They don't add value and they come off as rapport seeking. Instead of asking her where she's from, make a guess. She'll ask you why you guessed Arkansas, you'll give her a reason, and she'll giggle—whether you were right or not. (You *do* want her to contribute and invest in the conversation. But you want her to do so because she is attracted, not because you are forcing the conversation along with lots of questions. You must add value.)

- Be agreeable. You don't always have to be right. Don't take yourself too seriously. For example, don't use disagreement unless you need to enforce a frame. If you're arguing about something, you probably care too much. Remember why you're here.
- "Rapport" doesn't mean "boring." The vibe you created in the attract stage should still be simmering just below the surface. If it isn't, then you probably made M3 Sequencing Mistake #2: To Start in the Middle.
- Practice your **grounding routine,** which will be covered in this chapter.

REALLY—BE TALKATIVE

It's vitally important to be talkative. It's easy to say it, but actually try it for a few months of practice. If you have *so much* to talk about and you bombard her (or her set) with lots of fun and interesting conversation, showing humor, opinion, and passion, then you get to convey your personality.

The talkative person just gets laid *way* more often. The secret is to put

The Question Game

"Have you ever played the question game? Well, there are *rules.* . . .

"Rule One, you ask a question, then me, then you, and so on, back and forth.

"Rule Two, you have to tell the truth, the whole truth, and nothing but the truth. Like truth or dare but without the dare because I don't know how weird you really are." (Notice the neg.)

"Rule Three, you can't ask the same question that's already been asked.

"Rule Four, you have to ask questions that let skeletons out of the closet. Take advantage of our anonymity.

"Oh, and . . . Rule Five, you go first."

She will say, "That's not fair."

So you then ask, "How many boyfriends have you had?"

From here on, the question game will escalate sexually until she is asking you how often you masturbate. It's a fun routine. This is a comfort-building routine that's also useful for screening. Another great thing about the question game is that it can last for a really long time. When you get into C1, use this routine as your default.

Fun question: "Tell me a secret."

The Photo Routine

Preparation: Take pictures of yourself in interesting situations. Active shots–you doing fun things. Goofing off at your workout place. Rock climbing. Partying with male friends and girls. In midair while Rollerblading. The "bear shit" from the bear you bumped into while hiking. The best photos will convey value as well as your identity. Also include a couple boring or out-of-focus pictures for realism. Put these photos in a developing envelope, as though you just picked them up from the store where they were developed today and you just happen to have them with you.

Performance: While in set, use the envelope as a lock-in-prop on the target, while also demonstrating higher value to the set. If she tries to open the envelope, swat her hand and call her nosy. ("Jeez, is she always like this?" etc.) When the time comes to engage the target directly with A3 and C1, you can decide to "be nicer" to her and sit down with her to go through the pictures. For each picture, tell a story. During this time, you can demonstrate preselection, social proof, and other DHVs, build comfort, and also engage her in a fun dialogue where she contributes and invests. Your stories will remind her of her own stories, and she will tell one to you. Practice your spontaneous conversations. This way, you will always have a thread to go back to and a new story with each picture. The photo routine is one of the most powerful and versatile of all known Venusian arts gambits.

yourself in a talkative mood. Have you ever been in one? Close your eyes for a moment and remember what it was like at the time. Looking back on the women I have shared intimate moments with, I just talked their ears off on the path from meet to sex. After I witnessed positive body language and other IOIs, I would come out of the blue and say, "You're attracted to me." I don't talk about her. I don't ask many questions. I don't really expect her to have to say much at all. If she wants to join in, great, but otherwise, who cares? This is my world, and she is in it.

TALKING IS A LOGISTICAL TOOL

There is another benefit to talking—it occupies the conscious mind. Imagine that you're talking to your friend. You both get into his car, continuing your conversation, and he drives you to the beach. From your perspective, you were having this conversation, sights were flying by, and voilà! You're at the beach! It's like magic—the conversation was the opiate.

The pickup should be the same way. She is talking to you; everything feels so fun, comfortable, and natural. The conversation continues to flow—voilà! She's having sex. Like magic! You should constantly occupy her conscious mind.

Nothing ruins the mood like a long, quiet car ride back to the house . . . or a long, quiet walk back to the car. Talking and keeping the flow is necessary to overcome logistical difficulties that otherwise will arise.

COMMONALITY

People tend to be more attracted to those who they consider to be similar to them in some way. The more that you both have in common with each other, the more she will rationalize that this was **meant to be.**

She needs to be able to imagine you as a realistic addition to her everyday life. Sure, she enjoyed being entertained by you at the club, but compared to her home life, that's a circus. In real life, would the two of you *fit*? Would your respective social circles be compatible? Prepare

The Music Game

You proceed: I like . . . Pearl Jam. They're my favorite nineties band. Do you know the song "Garden"? I remember making out with my high-school crush to that song. Your turn.

Her: Okay . . . I like . . . Ray Charles. . . . I've always loved "Georgia on My Mind." Did you see that movie about him?

You: Yeah, I just saw that the other night in fact. He has one of the most beautiful voices I've ever heard. Wow, I'm kind of impressed. Ray Charles. I totally gave you insufficient credit. You have good taste in music. My turn. I love the band A Perfect Circle.

Her: I love Tool! I've been into them since their first CD.

You: No way, you like Tool? Not too many girls are into them. You know, I remember when their last CD came out. I was . . . [Tell a story] . . . So I never saw her again, but I still have that seashell she gave me when it rained. Your turn.

Don't credit her with great music taste on every band or song she gives you. Once in a while it's OK for you to say, "Oh, God, no. That song is shit compared to . . ." The pattern is this: If she gives you an answer, IOI her. If she doesn't, IOD her. After either, tell a DHV-spiked enriched story and then return to the question game with you asking the next compliance-testing question. This routine is best used as an opener on a single, in isolation with your target, or when you have her in your car or house on Day 2.

yourself by drawing out specific information from her in the comfort phase so that you can demonstrate commonality.

Be careful: If it looks like you're fishing for commonalities in an effort to ingratiate yourself with her, you look desperate. However, there are ways to share commonalities that aren't try-hard. For example, check out the classic MM music game.

CONSPIRACY

Imagine that you're gaming a girl. The two of you are sitting on a couch isolated from her friends, who are now out on the dance floor. You suggest a bounce next door for a piece of pizza.

Here on the couch you're someone she has just met and sat down to talk with for a few minutes. She's still here with her friends. But once the two of you step inside the pizza joint, you are there *together*. There is a powerful psychological effect.

Bouncing is covered in more detail in the next chapter. But what's interesting here is the shared frame. You and the girl are now in on something together. You have decided together to go on this journey together and now here you are together. Assuming you did your A3 properly, she has already been falling into your hoops and a "we are together" frame is now strengthening between the two of you.

Tip:
Have your pivot stop by and mention what a cute couple you and your target make.

This **shared reality** is known as a **conspiracy.** You can usually tell when people have a conspiracy together by the looks they give each other and by their use of **nicknames** and **inside jokes.** It goes without saying that you can also use these endearments to strengthen the conspiracy between you and your target. Be warned: This is exactly the sort of thing that would look try-hard if you were doing it too early in your set.

One easy way to create a conspiracy is to play games that involve you and the target having a secret together vis-à-vis someone else.

For example, girls love people watching. Try the Murder-Marry-Shag gambit.

VULNERABILITY

When people share vulnerabilities with each other, it demonstrates (and creates) an emotional connection between them. It's one of those things that, if done too soon, will come off like you are trying too hard to gain rapport with her—a DLV. So don't be Captain Sensitive when you first meet her. At the right time, however, sharing vulnerabilities is a powerful comfort builder.

Did she tell you something personal about herself? Did she tell you a secret? **The Question Game** is very useful for this sort of sharing. It's also possible to structure stories to make vulnerability appear as if it were revealed accidentally.

Here are some examples of field-tested vulnerability stories:

> The Murder-Marry-Shag Gambit
>
> As you put her on your arm, promenade-style, say, "OK, we're going to play a game called Murder-Marry-Shag. I will point out three guys in the crowd. You have to tell me which one you would murder, which one you would marry, and which one you would shag—and then you have to tell me why."
>
> After this happens, it's her turn. Continue walking around the venue together as she picks out three girls. Which one would you murder, which one would you marry, and which one would you shag? . . . And why?

+ An embarrassing story. Hint: *Cosmo Confessions* is a treasure trove of material.
+ First kiss experience (childhood regression).
+ Your pet died because you were too small to take care of it.
+ Your little niece fell down the stairs—"and I don't know what I would have done if things had gone bad that day, I love that little girl *so much!*"
+ The story of your father dying and you reaching closure.

Tell her about your childhood. Talk about the *cutest* little baby you just saw and how it reminded you of your little sister when you were a kid. Reveal an insecurity and then tell the story behind overcoming it. Tell her a secret. She'll be more likely to share one of her own.

Do **not** whine about your ex-girlfriend. And don't linger on sad emotions. "Pull" her sad strings and then move on to another one of your happier multiple threads.

So much unattractive behavior comes from a desire to avoid vulnerability. The secret is to embrace your vulnerability and still be unaffected by it. It's OK to be wrong. It's OK to laugh at yourself sometimes. Think about it: If you're sensitive about her seeing that you're wrong, then what she thinks obviously matters to you. But I thought you were unaffected? So the next time you tell the story of when you fought a lion with your bare hands, remember that it's more attractive—and interesting—to admit you were scared shitless than it is to play Mr. Tough Guy.

If that girl is going to be your girlfriend, she will eventually learn about your vulnerabilities anyway. Why wait until after sex to reveal them? Why not reveal them before sex, perhaps in the comfort stage?

PUNISHMENT / REWARD

You can't do a freeze-out unless she wants your attention in the first place. A takeaway done on someone who cares less isn't a takeaway at all. It only works when you are of value to her. When she says or does something negative, then *remove* your attention to make her feel lonely. She feels bad and knows she would prefer talking to you. That's why a freeze-out works.

Early in the set, when she's bad, tease her and frame-control. But in C1, don't go backward in the set. So give a slight IOD. Maybe stop talking to her for a moment, or turn away, or just barely shift your body language. It doesn't take much—women are very sensitive. Remember, you aren't communicating anger, merely a slight loss of interest.

In this way, the "punishment" is actually just a quick, sharp correction, like in dog training. It's not personal, and you're not angry.

Sometimes you just get caught up in your own reality and she doesn't always merit your full attention. So you turn away for a second, which indicates lack of interest, delivering a slight emotional tinge directly to her.

When you're training a dog to, say, not jump on you, don't hit its nose. That shows anger, and dogs often can't correlate your anger with their behavior. Simply detach yourself from the equation. Instead, take a dozen pennies and put them in a jar. Whenever your dog jumps up on you, shake the jar, which scares the dog.

Over time, however, your dog will come to recognize that *you* are doing it. Sure, it won't jump on you—but it also won't want to come *near* you again. It associates the uncomfortable emotion not to the bad behavior but to you.

The solution dog trainers have formulated is this proven procedure: After the correction for bad behavior, structure a challenge for the dog to do something *correctly*. Right after you shake the jar, say, "Sit," and help the dog sit. Then reward it with love and affection: "Goood girl!!!" "Yes, good boy!" If you *only punish*, the dog will see you as the punisher. If you want it to obey you and still love you, reward it as well.

Humans are the same way. That's why calling a girl on her shit while on the phone *sucks*. It just makes her not want to take your calls in the future.

Instead, when we correct a woman's misbehavior, we must then immediately structure an opportunity for her to jump through an easy hoop, thereby rewarding her for it. A "reward" statement might be, "Respect!" or, "Damn, that's witty; I give you that," or "OK, you win," or, "That was A-crowd!"

JEALOUSY PLOTLINES

For a girl, horniness is a less powerful motivator than jealousy. Which is better: a girl who feels horny but is in a club with her friends or a girl who isn't horny but is superjealous? Always choose **jealousy** in the club, because it is usually the moment when she realizes just how attracted she is to you. Horniness has its place, too, but *not* until you get her *alone* at the **sex location.**

A woman will not recognize just how valuable her S-and-R value-judging circuits have assessed you to be until she experiences an unexpected sense that she has lost access to that potential value. Imagine you're in the comfort phase, when you're not hitting on her but just hanging out and laughing together in C1, and another girl comes over and sits on your lap. You introduce the two and, voilà! Instant emotions! Now the target knows she in fact likes you. Before this moment, she simply didn't.

Plotlines must be built into your game consciously. In fact, negs are really a means of building a plotline between you and the target. The principle is that people are willing to work harder to preserve an existing investment than they are to make a new one, even if both carry exactly the same risk and reward. Simply put, **the fear of loss is a more powerful motivator than the anticipation of gain.**

The moment finally comes when you **choose her over the other girl.** This willingness to flake off girls (which they do to guys all the time) is a DHV. And for her, it is her moment of triumph over another woman, which she relishes. She has invested, she has experienced fear of loss, and now she has the prize: you!

The jealousy plotline gambit may sound Machiavellian, and perhaps it is. Just keep in mind that jealousy plots are extremely effective and women use them on men all the time.

Here's another way to use this: If you've already attracted a certain girl, but she isn't motivated enough to pursue you, just go into the next set and attract another girl. You may like the new one better and thus flake off the first one, or you may use the new girl as a pawn to make the first one jealous and finally recognize your value. You could even merge the two sets for greater technical maneuverability.

Value demonstration is the secret key to a woman. There's nothing better than a live demo to prove that there is another girl, that it's not just talk. After all, which is more powerful, telling a girl that other girls like you or actually having two girls on your arm? Telling a girl that you're adventurous or showing her a picture of you dangling off a cliff?

DEMONSTRATIONS THAT CREATE JEALOUSY

- Have a female wing or pivot who is "in the know" with you.
- Build a pawn while in the club.

For example, let's say I'm in isolation with my target and I do a brief takeaway. I'll use a lock-in prop on her (I enjoy using my cowboy hat) and then go find a girl from a previous set. I tell her, "I'm sitting over there with my friend; let me introduce you."

When I return with this female friend, this "friend" will sit on my lap. A previous set has now been merged with the new one, but instead of *group-to-group*, it's *isolation-to-isolation*, making a two-set.

From the point of view of the girl I brought over, introducing her to one of my other "friends" is respectful and a comfort-building tactic. That this friend is a hot girl helps with social proof. She also feels good when I kino her in front of the other girl.

My target—the girl who is still wearing my cowboy hat as a lock-in prop—now has a challenge on her hands, not to mention a completely unexpected trigger of **jealousy**. Boo-ya! Sometimes the first moment she feels jealousy is also the first moment she consciously realizes that she is into you and that she wants to have you, besting the other girl.

If you don't have ready pawns from previous sets, run off and enlist a girl to help you by saying, "I like this girl. Will you make her jealous for me?" It's a useful in-field tool.

If you have a pivot, tell her to find you and sit on your lap in two minutes. Or just game another set quickly, and then when

There are several ways to create a jealousy plot-line in-field:

- Find your pivot.
- Enlist a girl to directly help you.
- Backward-merge to a previous set. Introduce your girl to the previous target.
- Forward-merge by opening a new set and bringing your target with you.

you isolate the girl from that group, say, "I've got my friend over there; let me introduce you."

If you desire to game 10s specifically, know that you will *need* to practice **advanced group theory:** the art of merging groups. In my sets where my target was a 10 and where the jealousy plotline was performed, my success simply came more often. Make your targets jealous as part of your regular C1 or C2 game, and you'll have them wanting you.

Demonstrations are always more effective than verbal insinuations. Nonetheless, these verbal tactics can help you install jealousy:

While on the phone say, "Hold on; I have another call." Do this three or four times during the conversation and act annoyed. It'll make you seem popular. Girls have done this to me, and it works!

Also mention you have a girlfriend, whether you do or not: "A girlfriend of mine . . . ," or, "I don't think my girlfriend would like you flirting with me." Don't worry about blowing yourself out, because when the girl says, "I thought you had a girlfriend," you say, "Oh my God, you're attracted to me. I knew that would make you jealous."

After you make her jealous, it may increase your value and attractiveness to her, but she may hide her feelings and not respond immediately with visible IOIs. In fact, she may even be cold when you return to her. This is partly a congruence test, partly her pride on display. All you need to do is IOI her, and she will accept it. She can't help it now. She now knows she really likes you.

GROUNDING

I'm sure you've found yourself in a set when you reach the point where your target says, "What do you do?" You can give her your honest-but-lame answer like, "I'm a student," or, "I'm a system administrator," or, worse, try to circumvent the question entirely with, "I'm an ass model." A cocky answer like that might make her laugh initially, but she will probably ask you again soon enough. Do you have something to hide?

The problem is that you don't have an attractive **identity** or, if you do, it's not a strong one. Some guys will experiment with, "I'm a rock star," or, "I'm a promoter," or "I'm a public speaker," but your target either will think you're lying (in the same way we believe an "actress" is more likely a "waitress") or, if she *does* believe your evidence, become intimidated, weighing you down with her stereotype of you.

For example, I am a magician. How can she relate to that? So instead of answering her question with "I'm a magician," I can **ground** my present identity to her reality and harness the opportunity to convey a much richer personality. Here's how I do it:

+ "Well, when I was little I wanted to be . . ." (Childhood regression. Tell stories about my dreams and ambitions as a child.)
+ "When I was a teenager . . ." (Tell stories about how I got from childhood to what's next.)
+ "Now I'm a magician. Can you believe it?" (Talk about where I am now and what I'm working on next.)

Here is the applied format that I used to ground my identity to a recent 9's reality. It helped to attract her and build enough comfort to get her back to my place:

"What do I do? Well, when I was young . . . I wanted to be a ventriloquist, and then a magician. [Talk about this a bit.]
    "When I got a bit older . . .

+ Tell story of my first birthday party magic show and how the money was used to see a Copperfield show (five-minute story).
+ Tell story of how my biggest audience scared the shit out of me and how I went up and kicked ass. I really get into the fear of it all (three-minute story).
+ Talk about my first real TV experience (two-minute story).

 ◆ Tell her about moving to Las Vegas and why. This is a "vulnerability routine" in comfort stage (three minute story).

Tell her what is now on my plate: my **WTF?** underground Internet
show, my impending reality show on VH1, the book I'm writing,
and my seminars on various topics such as social dynamics and
wealth building (five minutes of stories). Tell her what I am planning on doing next: illusion-show concepts, publicity stunts, et
cetera (five minutes of stories).

That was more than twenty-three minutes of storytelling, and I was
holding this beautiful girl long before I performed any magic. The reason magic works for me, of course, is that I'm actually a magician. But
you don't need to use my style or perform magic yourself to use the
Mystery Method with great success. There's no shortage of former students of mine who don't perform magic yet by sticking to the method
and running their unique personality-conveying material still consistently attract women.

If I were to come in and just say, "I'm a magician," my target really
wouldn't feel that we share commonalities or lifestyle. She would have
to rely on stereotyping. I would also not appear very humble. She
would feel that I'm too different for her, and I would otherwise
overqualify myself. Some women, it seems, would actually reject a date
with George Clooney because they don't understand his lifestyle. They
feel they lack commonality, and this disparity creates discomfort. But
what if he gave such a woman his backstory and taught her what happened, step-by-step, as he became who he is today? This is the concept
of **grounding.**

By giving my target my backstory, I ground myself to her reality
("When I was a regular Joe") so that she can see how she, too, could be
the type of person I am now ("This is who I am today") if only she
were to make similar decisions along the way. You can even later use
this format to encourage your target to ground *her* life to *you* during

A2 by having her stick to the format. Simply ask, "Whoa, back up. So what happened next?"

Notice in my list of grounding stories earlier that the recurring theme is, "This is what led me to become who I am today." You, too, must do this—once you decide what your identity in fact *is*. Does this mean you must steal my magician identity in order to do the Mystery Method? No. You won't be telling stories of your first birthday party magic show (unless you in fact gave one). That would be a lie. You won't talk about how you learned the secret to a card trick by beating it out of a classmate of yours or how years later that classmate saw you on TV and said, "I can't believe your future changed that day." No, you won't use my specific material. But like me, you can use material based on your own real-life experiences. The format or game plan is the Mystery Method. The personalized *material* you use to fill in the format is what constitutes your own, personal style.

Now, how does one answer the deep question, "Who am I?" A friend of mine once told me, "You are what you repeatedly do," which is about as good of an answer as I've heard.

I do magic on a regular basis. I perform it almost every day, sometimes for beautiful women, sometimes for others. What do *you* do on a regular basis? Besides being a social butterfly, that is. Remember, the pickup arts exist to enrich your life, not define it. What stories do you already possess that convey who you have become today?

Grounding reality is far-reaching. It will change the *way* you do A2 and A3 and build comfort, but it will not alter their basic structure. It will also change the way you choose and structure routines, sequence them (that is, which routines you will use and when), and convey to your target the way you handle life's challenges.

So this is what you must now do to improve your game:

+ Figure out who *you* are by looking at what you *do* repeatedly—something you can say in a word or two (e.g., magician, writer, toy inventor, CEO, computer hacker, rock climber, rapper, public speaker, traveler . . . you get the idea). Are you really pursuing your dream? What would you do with your life if you had no chance of failure? Well, start doing it.

- Come up with several stories that convey how you went from being a normal kid to doing what you repeatedly do.
- Practice telling these stories to others to make the stories sound enthusiastic and natural. Listening, a woman should feel as though she's been on this journey with you.

While grounding, you can also ask her questions like, "So what were *you* like as a teenager?" This is a great way to open her up and get her invested in the interaction. But going for rapport in this way right at the opener would seem try-hard and telegraph interest. But now that she has given you IOIs and she has earned *your* IOIs, sparingly using questions in this way can help you build a strong connection with her.

REVIEW

- **The game is played in comfort.** It's necessary to develop a wide conversational rapport, a sense of comfort and trust, a sense that the interaction is real and genuine, and a feeling of connection.
- **Missing** elements of A3 and **comfort** are the primary reason that **girls will flake out** and blur when you call them the next day. Most guys get blurry numbers, or numbers that aren't solid, when they first start gaming.
- When you are **real** with a girl, it **creates trust** and allows her to feel safe. Don't front, sulk, or have a confrontational attitude. Keep it fun and remember that whatever the issue, **it's no big deal.**
- The **freeze-out** is the deliberate use of IODs to create discomfort (as **a way to train her** out of bad behavior). The freeze-out should come off sincere and inadvertent. She shouldn't perceive that you are *trying* to punish her; rather, she should sense

a slight lack of interest triggered by her behavior, resulting in a temporary loss of attention or validation.

+ A **comfort-building location** is usually a more quiet and secluded setting where you, your romantic interest, and perhaps a few friends can share lengthier dialogue.

+ The C1 location is a quiet spot somewhere within the meeting location. The C2 location is a place to go on a bounce, or time bridge. The C3 location is within the sex location.

+ It's important to be a talkative person and to practice your conversational skills constantly.

+ Practice **moving** her—take your romantic interest from the meeting location to the C1 location.

+ Be agreeable, don't ask a lot of questions, and remember: Don't seek attention, approval, or understanding from others. (**Be unaffected.**)

+ Don't get stuck on weird, creepy or stupid topics. Keep it fun, interesting, and emotionally compelling. (**Add value.**)

+ **Talking** is also a powerful logistical tool that keeps her conscious mind occupied and out of trouble while you advance the courtship. You don't want her **anti-slut defense** rearing its ugly head and screwing everything up.

+ Sharing **commonalities** builds comfort and rapport and helps her to imagine spending time with you in the future. Beware: Coming off like you're fishing for commonalities with her is a DLV. **Serendipity** must be preserved!

+ A **conspiracy** is a **shared frame** between you and your romantic interest, characterized by **inside jokes, nicknames,** and a growing **connection.** It is the natural outgrowth of the A3 process, where validation was used to bait her into frame submission.

+ **Vulnerability** is attractive and builds comfort. Instead of trying to protect your ego, set it free. Be willing to laugh at yourself. It shows confidence.

+ After you "**punish**" a girl with the freeze-out, give her a compliance test so that you can **reward** her for passing it.

+ **Jealousy** is a very powerful motivator. If she feels it, that's often when she first realizes that she wants you. This also gives her that much more **drama** when you do eventually **choose her.**

+ When we relate our identity, sometimes it can create distance instead of closeness. But the use of a **grounding** routine allows her to follow your life through stories, culminating in where you are today. This helps her relate to you and empathize as if she had been there with you.

+ Figure out what you *do* repeatedly. Pursue your dreams. To ground her reality to your identity, tell her stories that convey how you got to where you are today—and what's coming next.

....

MID-GAME AND END-GAME

*A sense that "it is on" between us . . .
logistical issues and the passage of
time . . . intimacy and seduction*

The point of C2 is to make the woman feel *familiar* with you. It's not about routines so much as **shared space**. Take her with you to the mall. Let her keep you company while you are working on a paper. It takes four to ten hours of comfort building to have sex with a girl. That's seven hours of babysitting, on average—just wait it out. When the time comes, get her isolated and escalate.

Mid-game is an opportunity to practice being with a girl and kissing her, to practice naturally leading her through bounces and bridges, to practice talking on the phone. Remember, **the Game is played in comfort.**

THE SEVEN-HOUR RULE

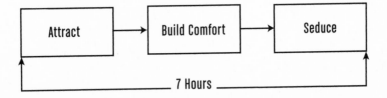

If you log the minutes you spend with a woman, you'll realize that it usually takes somewhere between four and ten hours, cumulatively, to go from meeting her to having sex with her. The average is around seven hours.

I discovered the **Seven-Hour Rule** while searching for patterns relating my success stories. Anecdotal evidence and field reports from many Venusian artists generally confirm the accuracy of the rule, excepting instances of **fool's mate** of course.

While it can take several days or even weeks to accumulate seven hours of time with a woman, if you seduce her prematurely you run the high risk of making her uncomfortable enough to have her attraction for you turn off.

I have also discovered that the most emotionally rewarding long-term relationships often develop into sexual ones within a week, sometimes within as little as a few days. However, this only happens when you accumulate an average of four to ten hours of comfort building in the presence of the woman before attempting to seduce her. My most passionate relationships (one of which lasted three and a half years) often became sexual within a few days of meeting the woman. They also averaged around seven hours in accumulated time before seduction occurred.

The following time log is a typical example of a modern-day courtship:

DAY	MINUTES	STAGE	LOCATION	HIGHLIGHTS
1	1:30	Attract, Comfort	Pub	Kiss, exchange numbers
3	0:05	Comfort	Phone	Invite for hot apple cider
4	0:10	Comfort	His Place	Brief house visit; then leave
4	1:15	Comfort	Café	Talk and hold hands
4	0:45	Comfort	His Place	Video, kiss, mall invite
7	0:15	Comfort	Her Car	Picked up to go to mall
7	3:00	Comfort	Mall	Meet at mall, share straw
7	0:25	Seduce	His Place	Bath and sex

Total = 7 hours and 25 minutes have accumulated in 7 days.

Most of the time you share with a woman should be invested in comfort building (mid-game) so that she will be comfortable when you begin seduction.

KISSING

Kino and kissing are comfort builders, not seduction.

+ If you go too far into seduction before you have enough comfort, you'll feel like a great player at the time, but you won't get the girl when (1) your fool's mate backfires and (2) she experiences buyer's remorse the next day.

+ How will you know the right moment to kiss? You must train your intuition through time in the field. A good rule of thumb is not to bother trying to kiss her until after she has given you three IOIs. For example: She touches you, she laughs at your jokes, and she picks up the conversation when you let it drop.

+ Consciously perform as many of the kiss gambits in this book in as many sets as you choose to. You will develop experiential social intelligence.

+ Within twenty minutes of meeting a woman, technically expect to be able to kiss her and isolate her for

Mystery's Kiss Gambit

You say, "Shh! You talk a lot. Would you like to kiss me?"

If she says yes, kiss her.

If she says, "Maybe," "Why?" "What do you mean?" or "I dunno," it means she would but is shy about it. Reply with a gleam in your eye, "Let's find out," and kiss her. Consider caressing the back of her neck to show you mean business, and abide by the 90/10 rule: You advance 90 percent of the way and she must advance 10 percent of the way to kiss you.

If she says no, reply, "I didn't say you could, punk; it just looked like you had something on your mind." (Don't ask, "Why not?" because it shows low self-esteem.)

If she says, "Not yet," or, "Not here," it means she's open to it, but there is a logistical issue (perhaps her friends are nearby). Say, "I understand," and know you can just maintain comfort and kiss her later in privacy.

comfort building. This doesn't mean that in the long term you should kiss every girl in every set, but you *should* have the *ability* to do so consistently.

✦ Trigger hardwired emotions. Control and direct each shared moment with her . . . for her. We are usually far too intellectual! Just tell the girl to *"shhh"* and nuzzle her. Put your mouth to her ear and inhale and whisper how good she smells. "I want to kiss you." Let the conversation drop. When she reinitiates, interrupt with, "Shh . . ." (**kiss**) "Kiss me," or, "You talk a lot. Would you like to kiss me?" or "Do you like having your neck bit? . . . Why? Because right now all I want to do is bite your neck," or "May I bite your neck?" If she says, "Why?" that means she wants you to. Only if she says, "No," do you *not* bite her neck. IOD, DHV, then repeat the gambit.

Practice for all contingencies.

Does it seem as if most of these lines involve asking her for permission to kiss her? Is that wimpy? They are just considerations. I've found that just going for the kiss without indicating your intentions can sometimes lead to embarrassment—more than her just saying no. It's much easier to save face from the situation when she says no than when you try to kiss her and she moves away.

That being said, feel free to field-test every kiss move you can think of. Just go right in for the kiss without saying a word. If she turns her head, use your hand to turn it back and kiss her anyway. Test it out a hundred times. Be enthusiastically willing to brainstorm and experiment.

THE C2 LOCATION: ANY COMFORT-BUILDING LOCATION SEPARATE FROM THE MEETING LOCATION AND THE SEX LOCATION

When you are in C1, the presence of your romantic interest's friends or family may at times compromise your comfort-building efforts. You may instead simply not have the time to sit with her. For whatever reason, when you are unable to continue building comfort in C1 you will have to jump from C1 to C2. Examples of C2 locations:

+ A bar, coffee shop, quiet restaurant, or living room
+ a mall or street where you are window-shopping
+ the walk or drive from one comfort-building location to another

Before you approach a woman in a meeting location, have your C2 comfort-building location preselected. Every successful pickup will inevitably jump to C2. You may jump from one C2 location to another as many times as necessary until you spend enough time and build enough comfort to shift successfully to C3.

JUMPING

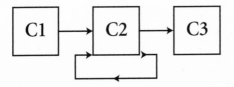

Going from one comfort location to another is called **jumping**. There are two ways to *jump*: the **bounce** and the **time bridge**. To bounce means to move your group of people to a different venue that same night. Time bridging is making plans to see her at another time.

The Bounce

One way to change comfort-building locations is *to do so at that time*. This instant venue change is called **bouncing**. (As when a friend says to you, "We're leaving for Mel's Diner. Let's bounce.")

In other words, the purpose of bouncing is to successfully transition you between comfort-building locations, so that you can continue spending time with your romantic interest **that same night**. Often these are in fact structured opportunities for the woman to pursue you! Examples:

* I turn to the woman I have been sitting with in C1 for a time and say, "My friends and I are about to grab a bite to eat over at Mel's Diner. You and your friends are more than welcome to tag along."

Daytime:
* "I'm starved; I've got to grab a bagel. Come join me."
* "I need to get an envelope from the post office. Come keep me company."
* "I'm going down to Melrose to grab a shirt I need to get. Let's go get some lunch."

Nighttime:
* "We're on the guest list for a better club. Come with us."
* "I'm starved. Let's get some food."
* "We're going next door to sit down for a bit. Would you and your friends like to join us?"

Bounce as often as needed. Be in any comfort location with your target for as long as necessary until you can finally bounce her to your place and move her into your bedroom. Just don't try to bounce too soon, or she won't yet feel safe enough to say yes. Bounces will generally succeed when you undertake them twenty-five to forty minutes into your set.

The best way to calibrate when to bounce is to just try it as often as possible. Your intuition will improve based on these experiences.

When you bounce, get her number first. That way you won't appear to be settling for the number later if the bounce doesn't work out.

The Time Bridge

The second way to jump comfort locations is *to agree to see each other at a later date.* This is called **time bridging**.

The so-called number close (as in, "I got her phone number") isn't even a close at all. There is only one type of close, really: **sex**. Are you a closer?

So what *is* a time bridge? A time bridge is an *optional* move in your game that you play *only* if you cannot follow the standard game plan of bouncing her for food and eventually sex. After all, if you both have the time and interest, isn't it better to continue *now* rather than try to continue it at another time?

But perhaps she won't bounce. Maybe logistics are screwed up, her friends are there, or you just haven't had the opportunity to build enough comfort for her to accept such an escalation. Then what? Well, you try to build as much comfort and trust as you can, and then you build a **time bridge**.

While talking, say, **"It would be cool to talk again sometime,"** and then, when she agrees, pop out the notepad and the pen as if *she* had requested it, saying, "Give me your number."

If your frame is congruent, she will behave as if it were her idea and comply. It all depends on the energy between the two of you. Is it on? When things are on, they just seem to flow so naturally. Instead of looking for clever ways to ask for her number, focus on creating that chemistry.

The purpose of the time bridge is simple: to bridge the gap of time that keeps you apart. You are with her **now,** and the time bridge will allow you to be with her again in person so that you may continue. Remember, the courtship goes from **meet to sex,** not from meet to phone number. Merely getting a number is *not* a bridge, because a bridge must have two sides. A number doesn't have a definite *other side.* When you call, you're stuck trying to set a date to see each other again. Had you done that in the first place, you wouldn't even *need* her number.

A time bridge leads to a definite time and place where you will be with her in person to continue the courtship. It is something that you have painted onto her imagination; perhaps you even ran a routine about it. In contrast, merely getting a number is nothing more than a stairway to heaven. It doesn't take much practice before you start getting phone numbers and realize they are all **blurring** or flaking out. Making those numbers more solid is a serious concern.

Try setting a **time and place** to meet up again. You should be prepared with two or three time bridges for situations when you can't bounce.

Some examples:

+ "I'm picking up some shoes at the mall tomorrow. Come keep me company and we can window-shop."
+ "I've got to drop off some stuff at my sister's. Come keep me company for the drive. I'll pick you up at eight P.M."
+ "I have a dinner party in two weeks. You *have* to come!"
+ "I'm going to the Magic Castle in Hollywood on Thursday to see a magic show. I'd like you to come. Let's exchange numbers."

Notice how you already have a *reason* to see each other in person again. If you just got the number, you could be in a position where you have to try to convince her to see you again. You don't even need to exchange numbers; it conforms too much to the stereotypical **dating frame.** If she won't meet you again, then you didn't build enough value and comfort in the first place—and the number wouldn't have changed that.

*Having solid game is more
important than getting phone
numbers. Solid game makes
for solid numbers.*

In the third example, you may get the number. (You've got two weeks to put together a dinner party!) Call her the next day and establish greater rapport over the phone. Time on the phone counts toward the seven hours—it's just another way of becoming a normal part of her life.

If you have enough comfort with her, you can meet her somewhere without even exchanging numbers and she will be there. But if you don't have enough comfort, the number will **blur,** which means it was worthless anyway. So don't place too much importance on getting numbers—practice **solid game.**

Choose locations that are conveniently near your house or where you plan on being anyways. Don't go out of your way to meet a girl who may flake on you. Have a life. The more compelling your life is, the more she will want to be a part of it.

Don't go to "coffee." Instead say, "I have to meet my friend

I went to a mall yesterday and sat beside an old man in the crowded food court with my "Made in Japan" meal. He started to talk to me about this and that: how skateboards used to be just metal wheels on wood boards and now they're fiberglass, and on and on. Well, I just wanted to eat my food, so I nodded but didn't want to invest in the conversation. (Nothing personal. He was a niceenough man and all, just . . . not my type, ha.)

I was displaying IODs to him. I didn't want to say, "Please don't talk to me," as that would have been rude and confrontational. But I averted my eyes from him, opened a magazine and flipped through it while he was talking, got really into my food, and answered his questions with one-liners.

Well, many women will find themselves in the same position I was in with that creepy guy. I'm not saying that you should give up on a girl when she gives you some IODs, because you can always turn it around, just as the old man could have talked about something that fascinated me and I maybe would have shared a conversation with him (a good reminder of how important it is to initiate an inherently interesting conversation). But imagine if this old man tried to get my number at the end of that conversation. Think how weird that would be.

I mean, I've gotten numbers from guys before. That's how we make male friends and buds. But imagine if this old man wanted to "hang out." I'd be like, "Um, no thanks." He's not offering any value, and I feel no connection to him. Asking for my number under those circumstances would be an attempt to force a familiarity between us, which is creepy, while simultaneously begging for rapport with me, which is try-hard. Both are severe DLVs.

I'm telling you this story because, as disturbing as it sounds, a lot of guys put women through the same thing: thirty seconds of boring talk and then hitting on the girl by asking for her number. Hot women are ultrasensitive to this–they've been through it a slew of times. So when you do attempt to construct a time bridge, make it natural. Have a reason to see each other again and play solid game.

Don't be the old man in this story.

Diane at the coffee pub to drop off a page layout for an underground newsletter. Meet me there."

PHONE GAME (FROM "MYSTERY'S LOUNGE"— LOVEDROP'S ORIGINAL ARTICLE ON PHONE GAME)

As you go into the field and practice your game, you will start to accumulate phone numbers. At some point the Venusian artist asks himself, "What do I do with these numbers? How do I convert these into lays?"

Oftentimes it happens like this: The Venusian artist has been in the field for any number of weeks or months and *finally* gets a number that has some importance to him. Perhaps the set went really well, or the girl is especially hot, or he hasn't been laid in a while. For whatever reason, he wants to play it *just right* so that he gets this girl. He might even post in an online forum or call a friend with game so he can ask, "What do I do with this number? How do I get this girl?" **He doesn't want to fuck this up!**

And there's the rub. You cannot ever let some number become that important to you—much in the same way that you cannot ever let any specific courtship matter to you. Opening sets and calling numbers are both activities that you should be doing over and over again purely for the practice.

If I am going into my sixth set of the night and I know there will be more sets tonight (and tomorrow night, etc.), I am not going to be that concerned about the outcome. Instead, I'm going to focus on the process and play with it. I can practice my skill while simultaneously giving off a natural, comfortable vibe with the subtext: *I don't care if I fuck this up.* Ironically, this results in a greater success rate.

The same must be true of your phone calls and dates (which to the Venusian artist are basically time bridges). You have to do many of them, or your skill will never improve. You can't take any one call or date seriously. You're just doing it for the practice. Enjoy the process. Be willing to lose and learn.

You shouldn't eject from a set immediately after getting the phone number. Stay around and talk for a few more minutes afterward. Otherwise you play into the pattern of all the other guys she flaked on who got her number immediately before parting.

Don't make the number itself the point. The point is the time bridge. Maybe the two of you discussed going to sushi or an art exhibit— whatever. The point is that the number is an incidental, not a goal. When in set, practice your bridging and collect numbers along the way.

Here are a few ideas to play around with on the phone:

- ✦ Don't assume that every phone call must occur for the purpose of setting up a meet. Is this how you use the phone when you talk to your friends? Get in the habit of going through your numbers and calling girls up just to chat or invite them to whatever fun activity you are currently doing.
- ✦ Call a girl up soon after the set is over (that same night) and chat for a few minutes, then let her go.
- ✦ Call her in the next day or two and chat her up, then let her go. In this way you come off nonneedy and you are conditioning her to accept you as a normal part of her life. Not some bar guy, not some club fantasy last Saturday—but **a real person who is a normal and regular part of her life.**
- ✦ Call her when you're somewhere fun, like you would call your guy friends, just to invite her over to hang out. Whether she

comes or not, you're having a good time without her and she knows it.

Time on the phone counts as comfort time (part of the seven hours). So use it as an opportunity to build comfort, become a pleasantly chatty person, and practice. Only time on the phone will give you the practice needed to vibe on the phone.

If you talk to her as described earlier, she will likely start hinting at a meet (especially if you talk about the fun activities and friends you experience in your day-to-day life). It's also perfectly reasonable to throw out an activity and see if she bites. If she doesn't, no big deal— your life is fun and fulfilling with or without her. You'll just get someone else. (This attitude, by the way, should be **subtext** to her, never explicitly communicated.)

Even if a girl hasn't accepted an offer to meet (or preferably made one of her own), it's **no big deal** to you because as soon as you get off the phone with her, you've still got to call five, ten, or twenty other girls and practice the same phone game with them. This is the most important piece of the puzzle. Holding that one phone number and worrying about fucking it up is going about it all wrong. You should be out gaming regularly to manifest a social circle of potential options. Eventually, you will be getting phone numbers regularly and you will be going through your calling rotation with equal regularity. **It's hard to be worried about any specific number when you know that you still have five others to call!** It's all just practice—and the lack of neediness will be evident in your voice.

A NOTE ON FLAKES

There will always be some percentage of flakes. Girls tend to be flaky creatures. They don't just flake on you—they flake on their friends and family, and often they even flake on themselves.

Just keep calling them anyway. **Put them in the rotation.** There is a random component to the game. Sometimes a girl who really liked you won't return your calls. Sometimes a girl who wasn't so solid is suddenly ready to come over and get it on. You never know! So just keep them in the rotation and keep practicing. Never take any number seriously. **As your game improves, your flake percentages will drop.** So keep working on value, attract, qualify, comfort, et cetera. Keep working on conditioning girls to chase you and get invested in the interaction. The tighter your game, the fewer flakes you will have to deal with.

Often you can't even get the girl on the phone. Big deal. Maybe it's **buyer's remorse.** Maybe her friends talked her out of it. Maybe her cat just died. Leave her a message and call the next girl. Go out practicing tonight. This is a lifestyle.

DATING (FROM "MYSTERY'S LOUNGE"— LOVEDROP'S ARTICLE ON DATING)

At some point in my game, I discovered that it was really easy to get isolated with a girl. I could game up a set, get a number, call her a few days later, and soon she would be sitting on my bed watching a movie with me.

But the problem was, I hadn't done enough A3 or comfort in order to escalate. There was this weird pressure for me to make a move, even though she wasn't ready for me to do so and even though it would be awkward—and then I'd never hear from her again. I discovered that I could get girls over at my place, but I couldn't make anything happen after that point.

The solution, for me, was to **design a specific date plan that I could repeat over and over again**—a routine I could practice on many different girls until I had my dating game tight. If you're getting numbers but not lays, it's useful to practice your dating game in a structured way.

When designing my date, I decided it should have as many venue changes, and as many hours together, as possible. Moving and bouncing are powerful comfort builders, so I built these ideas into my date routine. Here's what I came up with:

- (On the phone) "Let's do sushi Wednesday night like we talked about. There's a good place near where I live. Come by around seven and we'll go eat."
- 7:30 P.M. Girl shows up at my place. I come downstairs, but I "forgot" something, so we have to run back upstairs "real quick." She gets to see my pimp pad and my bay view, which she oohs and ahhs over. Then I hustle her out and we drive to the sushi shop. Kudos to David DeAngelo of *Double Your Dating* for this trick. It familiarizes her with your place so that it's not a **big deal/fear of the unknown** when you return! Better still, it makes her more curious about being in your apartment since you hustled her out.
- 8:00 P.M. We're at the sushi shop. I have various routines that I always do . . . "can't pour your own sake," Japanese voice stuff, teach her chopsticks, et cetera. The specifics aren't important. Most of the time here is vibing, practicing comfort, the question game, palm-reading, whatever. Getting to know each other.
- 9:00 P.M. "There's this really cool band playing across the street—let's go check it out!" There's an eighties parody rock band that plays every Wednesday right across the street from this sushi shop. I have a VIP card to the venue, so we don't have to wait in line. I take the girl across the street, but the band hasn't started yet. So we have a few drinks and more comfort-building material, along with some push-pull to keep up the sexual tension.
- 10:00 P.M. The concert room opens and we enter (another venue change). As the crowd thickens, either I'm leading her through the crowd or I've got my arms around her for protection. The band goes on shortly after that, and she spends the next two hours either laughing at their comedic dialogues or singing along with old favorite rock songs.
- Midnight. We drive back to my place. I say, "OK, you can come upstairs, but only for a few minutes. I have to work tomorrow."
- 12:30 A.M. We're sitting on my balcony making out. I take her

by the hand, say, "Let's go make out like a couple of teenagers," and lead her back into my bedroom and fuck her. Notice how this routine allows me to get in lots of venue changes, pass time with the girl, and also practice other bits of my game. When I need to attract, I can be cocky and playful and use hot-cold dynamics. I can keep screening and qualifying her, and I can work on comfort building and kino escalation. This all occurs within a date structure that I can repeat every week with a new girl and practice until it is tight. And tight it is—this routine gets me laid.

Here's another date routine that I came up with recently for Saturday afternoons:

- 10:30 A.M. "It's such a beautiful day. I'm going to get lunch at the beach near where I live. Come over and we'll go together."
- 12:00 P.M. Let her come upstairs briefly and then hustle her out. Drive to the main drag and park.
- 12:15 P.M. There's a billiards place that serves food. We hang out here for an hour or two, eat lunch, and shoot some pool. Meanwhile, I continue gaming, comfort building, et cetera.
- 2:00 P.M. Bounce and walk up and down the street. Go into clothes shops and try on stuff. There's one shop in particular with cool masks, wigs, et cetera. Go into a vintage shop and try on more stuff.
- 4:00 P.M. After a few hours of bouncing around together, we go back to my car.
- 4:15 P.M. Swing by the store on the way home "to pick up some stuff." Get barbecue fixings. Walking around in the store together is a great way to subconsciously activate domestic couple fantasies in her brain. She also gets involved in picking food out, which involves her in the barbecue at my place.
- 5:00 P.M. Get back to my place. Make a few drinks and fire up the barbecue. Watch the sunset together. Make out, et cetera.

Notice that all the venue changes seem perfectly spontaneous to her, even though they've all been planned out. So her experience is fun, constantly changing, and without pressure. You are leading through all of this and practicing your date game along the way.

Design a date plan (or several) that you can execute over and over again. Build the most useful logistics into the date. Design in the seven hours. Design in the venue changes. Design it so she ends up at your place.

Do it over and over again with many girls. Focus on improving your skill and improving your dating routine. Don't take it too seriously.

THE C3 LOCATION: ANY COMFORT-BUILDING LOCATION WITHIN THE SEX LOCATION

Not until you have built enough comfort with a woman can you jump to C3. Examples of C3 locations:

+ Couch in your living room
+ Whirlpool a short distance from your bedroom or hotel room
+ Couch in lobby near your hotel room

Since every successful courtship will inevitably lead to the C3 location or the sex location, take efforts to secure a C3 comfort-building location before you even approach a woman in a meeting location.

THE SEX LOCATION

Most meeting locations, including many of those for comfort building, are inappropriate settings for sexual intimacy. So participating in a mutual seduction will require jumping to a sex location.

A sex location is marked primarily by its privacy. It should also be in close proximity to a C3 comfort-building location, so that you have only a short distance to move when the time comes. For example, your bedroom is very near your living room.

The best seduction location is one that allows you complete control, such as the bedroom of your own apartment or house. Here few variables (phone calls, roommates, parents, pets, etc.) can impede your success.

Consider the various benefits and limitations of the following sex locations:

+ A vehicle
+ A hotel room
+ A friend's living room or bedroom
+ The woman's bedroom
+ Your bedroom

Some C3 comfort-building locations, such as a private living room, may also be good sex locations. If you are in such a location, you can save yourself from having to move from C3 to the sex location.

Secure a sex location before approaching a woman in a meeting location. Don't leave the success of your end-game to chance.

MOVING FROM C3 TO S1

I'm in my living room with a woman, showing her some short comedic home movies. We're in C3. I put on some music and light up the hookah and we share smoking it. I inhale the smoke from the pipe and then exhale it into her mouth. We do this several times.

Sharing intimacy by holding each other and kissing, we now progress from kissing into foreplay. We're both aroused as I take her by the hand, lead her into my bedroom, hand her a box of matches, and say, "Here. Light the candles while I find the incense." Then I say, "Can you close the blinds for us? I'm going to wash up." A minute later, I return. "Why don't you go wash up while I light the incense," I say to her, pointing out where the bathroom is.

Building the seduction scene together in this way is similar to the way long-term couples regularly do it. Such ritualistic behavior is familiar and comfortable.

Caveat: Do not make this move until you have properly qualified and built comfort with her. If you do, it will activate her **anti-slut defense,** cause her to get **buyer's remorse,** or do both.

Further complicating matters, if the window of opportunity is open and you miss it, don't expect it to open twice for the same bird; it seldom does. For example, she may go home and backward-rationalize all the reasons that it didn't happen. In the interests of practice and rapid improvement, when in doubt attempt to escalate. Even if you're wrong, it will still improve your calibration.

S2: LAST-MINUTE RESISTANCE

Every woman has hardwired into her head a behavioral circuit that works to protect her from getting pregnant by a man who has no intention of sticking around to help raise the child. The resistant behavior this emotive circuit elicits right before first-time sex is called **last-minute resistance.** It is your job to ease her through this uncomfortable emotion should it arise. Having sex carries a much larger risk and investment for a woman than it does for a man from an evolutionary perspective. **Last-minute resistance** is her last line of defense before the point of no return.

A woman's **LMR threshold** may differ from person to person, and a woman's own LMR threshold will change depending on the value of the man she is about to sleep with and other circumstances. Here are some common trigger points:

+ Kissing
+ Touching breasts
+ Top removal

+ Bra removal
+ Pants removal
+ Panties removal
+ Fingering
+ Oral sex (giving or receiving)

OVERCOMING LAST-MINUTE RESISTANCE

"You've Hijacked My Brain . . ."

Your romantic interest may not feel qualified enough for you. She may believe that if she gives it up too easily, you will simply move on afterward. This is why it's so important in A3 that she feels her efforts are succeeding and that she is winning you over. If this is missing, girls will freak out just prior to sex and say, "Why me? Why do you like me?" or, "I don't even know you. . . ." If you say, "Baby, I just can't stop thinking about you," this would inoculate against her LMR, but only if it were said hours earlier in C2. Say that while in bed with her and you could be lying to get her to submit to you. Instead, repeatedly convey to her throughout the three comfort phases that your brain has been highjacked, that you can't help but think of her constantly, and that the feeling is growing stronger and stronger. Don't creep her out and stalk her. Just tell her she is on your mind more often than you thought possible and it concerns you a bit.

"We Should Stop . . ."

The primary technique in the LMR arsenal is **token resistance,** *usually verbal in nature while the physical simultaneously continues to escalate.* She may say, "Baby, we should slow this down." What is the purpose of this?

The ideal scenario involves growing sexual tension that, at some point, triggers a loss of all control (and therefore accountability). She cannot help but be ravenously taken. **It's not her fault.** A force overtook her utterly beyond her control: the force of nature. Token resistance is necessary to make that feeling real. *If you don't resist, she will.*

Notice that if *she* gives token resistance, the best response is to just agree with her and even echo it. If you disagree, you are only giving her something to push against. Don't give her **traction** by way of disagreement.

If you're undressing her and she says, "We should stop," just agree with her . . . and then keep going. "I know, baby," you reply as you continue to undress her. "We should stop."

PLAY SOLID GAME

Her emotional circuitry is designed to select for a high-value man whom she trusts and with whom she pair-bonds. If your game is tight, last-minute resistance will be greatly reduced as an issue. So examine your basic game:

+ Are you a healthy, ambitious, socially comfortable person?
+ Do you convey a lack of neediness at all times?
+ Have you otherwise demonstrated value via preselection, the leader-of-men switch (social intelligence and social proof), emotional stimulation, frame control, and so on?
+ Has she chased and otherwise invested in the interaction?
+ Have you been compliance testing? Do you have kino escalation and compliance?
+ Does she feel that she has earned your interest? (Have you demonstrated your "growing pair bond" for her, using qualifiers and other IOIs?)
+ Have you built comfort and trust, and a sense of connection, over seven hours and several venue changes? Did you use the jealousy plotline so she is sure she wants you?

FREEZE-OUTS

If last-minute resistance seems insurmountable, do a freeze-out: Turn on the light, snuff out the candle, check your e-mail, head to the kitchen to make a sandwich, or pull out a checkerboard and challenge her to a game. The power of this is in its sincere delivery. If you were sulking or angry, that would show that you were affected. Just act as if your arousal circuitry has simply been shut off. She will feel the sense of loss and will allow herself to raise her LMR threshold level.

S3: SEX

Having sex with a woman for the first time is what you've been waiting for, the culmination of your efforts, the payoff for your Venusian arts mastery. To use the martial arts analogy from chapter 3, Bruce Lee trained for a reason; eventually, it was time to get in the ring. Yet going to bed is more than just a successful conclusion to courtship that is the hallmark of the Mystery Method. Seduction also opens a new door to the beginning of the next phase of your relationship with the woman.

The focus during your first sexual encounter should be on making her comfortable, having fun and playing, and taking your connection to a higher level. Unless the two of you share a mutually agreed-upon interest, save the freaky stuff for later. When you're slowly undressing her for the first time, whisper in her ear how beautiful she looks bathed in candlelight—don't ask if she's into anal sex or if you can tie her up to the bedpost. During that first encounter, definitely keep the whips and chains in your toy box.

Practicing safe sex is always incredibly important, but particularly so during your first encounter with a woman. Be sure to use protection, for your sake and hers. Being irresponsible during an initial sexual encounter is hardly a prescription for building mutual trust. What's more, if you're irresponsible and acquire a communicable disease in the process, your gaming will be severely curtailed. That's the best-case scenario, too. Needless to say, unprotected partners can even put each other's lives in jeopardy. Nothing is worth that risk.

By carefully choosing your target in the field and then confirming the validity of your choice through the attraction, comfort-building, and seduction phases you will have selected a woman of such beauty and quality that you will want to have sex with her many times. In chapter 1, I mentioned Wilt Chamberlain's scoring record—no, not one hundred points in one game but twenty thousand women in his bed. Later in life, however, he famously said that he would have preferred sleeping with one woman twenty thousand times. Yes, it was probably bullshit. But it does give you the sense that even a prodigious Venusian artist like Wilt the Stilt ultimately understood that at some level sexual fulfillment involves more than fucking someone once. There's also the high that comes from getting a phone message from the woman telling you what a wonderful time she had, not to mention the feeling that comes from subsequent encounters that feel even more erotic than the first one because you're both more comfortable with each other.

If you have sex with the woman only once and disappear, when she wants you to stay in her life in some capacity, a protection circuit in her head will punish her, sometimes severely, for compromising her chances of survival and replication. I've been told that it feels to a woman as if something very important has been stolen from her, and it's unethical to subject anyone to such painful and regretful feelings.

REVIEW

- It usually takes four to ten hours of comfort building before a woman is ready to have sex. This is known as the **Seven-Hour Rule.**
- Kissing is a comfort builder. Through practice it is possible to isolate and kiss girls consistently within twenty minutes of opening the set.
- The **C2 location** is any comfort-building location separate from the meeting location and the sex location.
- Going from one comfort location to another is called **jumping.** There are two ways to jump: the **bounce** and the **time bridge.**
- **Bouncing** is the act of leaving one venue and going to another one *at that time.*

- If you bounce, get her number first. That way you won't appear to be settling for the number later if the bounce doesn't work out.

- A **time bridge** is an agreement to see each other at a later date. This is an optional move in your game that you play only if you cannot follow the standard game plan of bouncing her for food and eventually sex.

- Having solid game is more important than getting numbers. Solid game makes for solid numbers.

- It's important to be practicing your game and getting lots of phone numbers. When you have five or ten numbers to call, you are much less likely to worry about *fucking it up*. No single number ever becomes that important to you, which is exactly the right attitude.

- After you get her phone number, stay and talk for a few more minutes.

- Get in the habit of going through your numbers and calling girls up just to chat or invite them to whatever fun activity you are currently doing.

- Many girls will flake when you call them. It's **no big deal.** Just keep working on your game and keep up on your calling rotation. The Game is a combination of skill (which requires practice) and luck (which requires random chance). Both are greatly increased by playing the numbers.

- If you are getting numbers but not sex, it's useful to practice dating in a structured way. Design a date plan that you can repeat over and over again for the practice.

- Build the most useful logistics into the date. Design in the seven hours. Design in the venue changes. Design it so she ends up at your place.

- The **C3 location** is any comfort-building location within the sex location, such as your living room or Jacuzzi.

- A **sex location** is marked primarily by its privacy and should be in close proximity to a C3 location. Usually this is your bedroom.

- Once you go from C3 into S1 (foreplay), you have crossed the point of no return. She will get **buyer's remorse** if you do this too soon, before enough comfort has been built.
- **Last-minute resistance** is a fear that women experience just prior to having sex, similar to the way that men experience approach anxiety. It is your responsibility to ease her through this.
- Often last-minute resistance is greatly increased as a result of weaknesses in your game. By improving your game, you also reduce last-minute resistance as an issue.
- Other techniques for combating last-minute resistance are **token resistance, playing solid game,** and **persistence freeze-outs.**

CONCLUSION

....

GO FORTH AND CONQUER

Thanks for joining me on the journey to becoming a pickup artist. Having read this book, you are now armed with some of the best information, tactics, strategies, and knowledge that the Venusian arts community has to offer. I feel privileged to have shared it with you.

Of course, it's one thing to read something, but putting the Venusian arts into practice is quite another matter, especially given the remarkable unpredictability of human social interactions and responses. (Think of it in terms of the difference between reading a how-to manual on sex and actually making love to a woman.) That's why I can't overstate the importance of getting out in the field and honing your gaming skills through constant practice in real time on live targets.

To use a sports analogy, an all-star athlete didn't get that way overnight—he spent years in an empty gym, throwing footballs, kicking soccer balls, running laps, whatever his art required. LeBron James, for example, a top basketball player, practiced the various aspects of his game for years so that when the time came in a game to hit a crucial shot with the shot clock expiring, the crowd roaring, and three defenders jumping toward him, he would know exactly what to do. Through endless repetitions, he has calibrated his game to an incredibly sophisticated degree, in the terminology of the Venusian arts.

Same thing with me and other "all-star" pickup artists: We practiced until we perfected our craft. As with LeBron on the court, I will encounter little in the field that will faze me, because I've seen everything and practiced for it all already. He needs to move past obstacles, often with the help of wing players, in order to hit his target and score. Same with me.

But no matter how many times you score in the game of pickup, what's most amazing is what you learn about yourself along the way. As you remove obstacles in the field, you'll find it much easier to surmount obstacles in every other aspect of your life, including your profession, your finances—actually, you name it. Let me put it this way: If I'm able to disarm two or three obstacles and pick up a completely unapproachable supermodel in a club, do you think I'm going to be fazed when buying property or dealing with a difficult person in some sort of transaction? Not even.

Along with practicing pickup on your own, make sure to engage in continuing education, because there is always much to learn. (In fact, I learn new things about pickup every day, which is why I systematically update my own methodology every six months.) I give MM seminars, workshops, and boot camps, and if you can't make it to those, I've compiled a five-DVD companion to this book titled *Mystery's Video Archive*, which will show you these techniques being used in the field by me and other Venusian artists. You can find out about these products and services and more by visiting mysterymethod.com.

Until then, game on!

GLOSSARY

Accomplishment introduction: The wing describing the pickup artist to the set for the first time in a way that conveys not only his name but also something impressive that he has done (e.g., "This is Mystery. He levitated over Niagara Falls").

Advanced group theory: The art of merging groups in the field.

Average frustrated chump (AFC): An armchair pickup artist who is actually just a nice guy with a tendency to place women on a pedestal, only to have them walk all over him. Rarely closes his targets.

Anti-slut defense (ASD): A highly calibrated circuit in women used as an interrupt mechanism to avoid having others *perceive* them as a slut, as well as to avoid the discomfort of *feeling* this themselves.

Approach anxiety: The urge to run away from a woman possessing high replication value, even in the presence of an equally overwhelming urge to mate with her.

Approach invitations: Eye contact and other acts suggesting that a woman wants you to be proximate to her physical space.

Arbitrary target: Someone gamed for the sake of practice rather than as a result of physical attraction.

Bait-hook-reel-release: A metaphor describing the application of compliance testing, screening, qualifiers, and other aspects of A3.

Blurring: The tendency of women in the field to give out phone numbers that don't work. Numbers that do work are called solid.

Body rocking: The use of physical movement to suggest you're about to leave the set.

Bounce: You and the girl changing venues together.

Buyer's remorse: The feeling of regret a woman experiences when, after foreplay but before sex, she feels she has been pushed or, on her own, gone too far too soon.

Calibration: Social intuition, finely tuned from time spent in the field, allowing Venusian artists to predict social behavior before it occurs.

Canned material: A particular value-demonstrating routine that has been internalized and is ready for use in set. Such a routine is said to be in the can.

Cat theory: Keeping "bait" just out of a woman's reach and continually enticing her in small increments. She must be baited to chase like a cat with a string.

Comfort-building location: A quiet, secluded setting where you, your romantic interest, and perhaps a few friends can share in lengthier dialogue.

Compliance momentum: The process of having the target jump into progressively larger and more frequent hoops. Negative compliance momentum is the opposite.

Compliance testing: Asking a target to do something in order to gauge her interest in you.

Compliance threshold: The point along a continuum separating those tests she will and will not undertake when asked.

Congruence testing: Conscious or unconscious screening by women in the field to determine if a man will be able to adequately support and protect her and her offspring.

Consistency principle: A woman's tendency to be consistent with the behavior and frame to which she is already accustomed when interacting with you.

For example, if she didn't object to your touch by the time you withdrew it one time, she likely won't the next.

Conspiracy: A shared frame between you and your romantic interest, characterized by inside jokes, nicknames, and a growing connection.

Courtship: The process of beginning a sexual relationship. "From meet to sex."

Cutting the thread: Ending a conversational thread that is no longer useful to your purposes and introducing a new thread to replace it.

Decimal rating scale: Scoring female targets based solely on their physical appearance, with 6 representing an OK girl and 10 a supermodel. Pickup artists don't bother with anything below a 6.

Demonstration of higher value: Anything that conveys higher S-and-R value.

Demonstration of lower value: Anything that conveys lower S-and-R value.

Disarm: To temporarily remove yourself as a threat in the eyes of the target's friends by negging her.

Discretion: Not bragging about sexual conquests. Makes women more likely to indulge in a sexual adventure that they trust holds no social consequences.

Dynamic social homeostasis: The state of perfect balance all social animals seek to achieve between protecting themselves from and aligning themselves with others.

Emotional stimulation: Getting a woman to respond to something just because it "feels right," even if it doesn't necessarily make sense. The opposite of rational discourse.

End-game: The third and final stage of courtship.

Engine of survival: Nature's long-established emphasis on replicating as the prerequisite to all species on earth surviving and evolving.

External interrupt: An abrupt change in the internal dynamic of a set, often caused by someone else's arrival.

False disqualifier: A line that has a disarming effect on the target while demonstrating confidence, fun, a lack of neediness, and a discriminating attitude.

False time constraint: The carefully cultivated illusion in your target's mind that you are about to leave.

Fool's mate: Seduction-first tactics. Typically only works on girls who are drunk or extremely horny. Success becomes increasingly less probable the more socially experienced the woman is.

Fool's mate fantasy: A seducer who expects to meet a woman and then take her to a bathroom stall or somewhere similar for sex as part of fool's mate. Not considered solid game.

Frame: The underlying meaning, the context, the implication, the unspoken assumption, in everything you say. The frame supplies meaning to the content.

Frame games: The behavioral cues and subtleties through which people convey their assumptions.

Freeze-out: The deliberate use of indicators of disinterest to create discomfort, as a way to train a woman out of bad behavior.

Friend: One who fears expressing his romantic intent to a woman he has spent time attracting and getting to know.

Friendship zone: A trap that occurs when a woman grows so used to someone's nonsexual comfort building that she prefers him to stay that way. If she says, "Let's just be friends," you're there.

Gaming locations: Places where you and your romantic interest will likely visit during courtship.

Great collapse: Sickness, poverty, loneliness resulting from unbridled spiraling.

Grounding: Giving a target the backstory to your current reality so that she can identify more closely with it.

Group theory: The application of social dynamics and the M3 Model to collections of people found in public settings.

Having standards: Subtle cues in your behavior setting the frame that you are a selective, high-value guy.

Hierarchy of needs: Abraham Maslow's theory stating that human beings are motivated by unsatisfied needs and that certain lower needs must be satisfied before higher needs.

Hired gun: A woman employed by the management of a meeting location for her beauty. Examples include hostesses, shooter girls, and promotional models.

Hoop: Something a person produces or asks to see if you will "jump" for him or her.

Incongruence: A disconnect between what you say and how you say it.

Indicators of disinterest (IODs): Signs, mostly nonverbal, that a woman isn't attracted to you.

Indicators of interest (IOIs): Signs, mostly nonverbal, that a woman is attracted to you. These can be "passive" (things she doesn't do) "active" (things she does), or even "fake."

Inner game: The internal strength of your frame.

Internalization: The process of practicing the skill set of the Mystery Method until it becomes automatic.

Investment: The extent to which a woman involves herself with you. The investment can be financial, temporal, emotional, exertional, et cetera.

Kino: Physical touching of any kind. Short for "kinesthetic."

Kino escalation: Progressively more intimate physical contact.

Kino pinging: An expression of growing attraction between two people that starts with verbal jousting back and forth and escalates to light, playful pushing.

Last-minute resistance (LMR): A woman's resistant behavior toward first-time sex once it becomes imminent. Her last line of defense.

LMR threshold: The dividing line between a woman having and not having sex with you. Varies from encounter to encounter.

Leader of men: An attraction switch turned on in women when they see a man leading other men.

Lock-in prop: Something tangible (e.g., a hat, a scarf) handed to the target to make it more complicated and harder for her to leave the set.

M3 Model: The part of the Mystery Method that describes courtship from when a man and woman meet until the beginning of their sexual relationship.

Martial arts: The arts of self-defense, which aids in survival.

Meeting location: Any place that offers a high probability of meeting women. The number of women available for gaming can make a location either "target rich" or "target poor."

Merge backward: To reopen a previous set and merge your existing set back into it.

Merge forward: To open a new set and merge your existing set into it.

Mid-game: The middle stage of courtship.

Move: Relocating a girl to a different area of the current venue.

Moxie: Inventive courage, allowing the Venusian artist to always lead the interaction.

Multiple conversational threads: Talking in a nonlinear fashion, as close friends do. Doing the same with someone new creates the feeling that you and she are already old friends.

Naturalization phase: The length of practice time it takes for a scripted routine to come out congruently.

Neg: A subtle-yet-negative statement that puts a target off-guard and makes her question her own value, increasing yours on a relative basis.

Nice guy: A man who seek comforts with a woman before generating attraction.

Obstacle: A friend of your target.

Opener: A short story or comment used to get a group's attention and earn their acceptance of your presence. These can be "direct," such as telling the target that she's beautiful (not recommended), or "indirect," whereby the target remains ignorant of your interest in her (recommended).

Orbiter: A nice guy who poses as a hot woman's friend but secretly wants to fuck her.

Pawn: A girl whom you have gamed previously for the express purpose of bringing her into your next set, so that it will open easier. Often used to lower protection shields.

Peacocking: Wearing outlandish clothes in the field to advertise your survival abilities to women. Being unaffected by the social pressure that this creates demonstrates higher value.

Pecking: The act of leaning in every time the target says something. Do not do this!

Pickup: The first stage of courtship.

Plausible deniability: Giving a woman the sense that anything that might happen is "on you," not her. It's "not her fault."

Player traps: There are three: (1) failure to justify a mutual attraction, (2) disregard of comfort, and (3) buyer's remorse.

Preselection: An attraction switch that gets triggered when a woman sees you have already been preapproved by other women.

Protection shield: Certain strategies, built up over time, that collectively enable women to avoid constant approaches from men.

Proximity: Physical nearness. Often an indicator of interest.

Rationalization: Mental processes used by women to justify their actions, whether it's cheating on their boyfriends without feeling guilty or going out "just to dance" when their emotional circuitry is actually compelling them to seek replication.

Replication: Passing along one's genes to offspring.

Routine stack: A sequence of canned material—an opener, a few routines, some gambits, and so on—for use in the field.

Seducers: Inexperienced pickup artists who focus on having sex with a woman *before* attracting her.

Seven-Hour Rule, The: The average length of cumulative comfort building it takes before a woman is ready for seduction.

Sex location: The place, usually a bedroom or hotel room, where the pickup artist and his target engage in intercourse and other forms of intimate contact.

Social alignments: Friendships and other relationships formed by people to improve their chances of survival and replication.

Social hook point: The threshold at which the pickup artist has demonstrated sufficiently high value to become part of a set.

Social proof: Showing that others value you highly. Conversely, one can have negative social proof.

Social robot: One who lacks the ability to vibe naturally with people.

Solid game: Picking up targets following the steps that constitute the Mystery Method. Opposite of fool's mate.

Spiraling: The runaway chain reaction that can be triggered when at least one vital area of focus is neglected for too long.

Statement of interest: An explicit verbal statement making clear your growing interest in a target.

Sticking points: The parts of a Venusian artist's game that are giving him trouble.

Subtext: Something implied through indirect means.

Survival: Living, as opposed to dying.

Three-Second Rule: States that a Venusian artist must open a woman's set within three seconds of spotting her in the absence of extenuating circumstances (e.g., the presence of a waitress). The artist should also be in set within three seconds of first entering the venue.

Time bridge: Exchanging contact information to continue gaming the target at a later time and different place.

Token resistance: Temporarily hesitating to escalate physical contact. It's a programmed emotional response in women to avoid feeling like a slut.

Try-hard: Investing too much visible or palpable effort in demonstrating value.

Venusian arts: The art of picking up a woman you just met and successfully embarking upon an intimate relationship with her, which aids in replication. Practitioners are called Venusian artists.

Vital areas of focus: Health, wealth, and love—the three things that must be satisfied to fulfill one's purpose in life and ensure survival and replication.

Waypoint: The moment, usually three to five minutes in, when you ask a set, "So how do you all know each other?" Also used to describe points in the Game, such as opening or isolating, that must always be present in any set that leads to sex.

Wing: A companion of the pickup artist whose primary purpose is to help him get his target.